Sod That!

Sod That!

···

103 Things NOT to Do
Before You Die

SAM JORDISON

Copyright © Sam Jordison 2008

The right of Sam Jordison to be identified as
the author of this work has been asserted by him in accordance with the
Copyright, Designs and Patents Act 1988.

First published in hardback in Great Britain in 2008 by
Orion Books
an imprint of the Orion Publishing Group Ltd
Orion House, 5 Upper St Martin's Lane,
London WC2H 9EA

An Hachette Livre UK Company

1 3 5 7 9 10 8 6 4 2

A CIP catalogue record for this book is available
from the British Library.

ISBN: 978 1 4091 0055 3

Designed by Bryony Newhouse
Illustrations by Peter Mac

Printed in Great Britain by Clays Ltd, St Ives plc

The Orion Publishing Group's policy is to use papers that are natural, renewable
and recyclable and made from wood grown in sustainable forests. The logging
and manufacturing processes are expected to conform to the environmental
regulations of the country of origin.

Every effort has been made to fulfil requirements with regard to reproducing
copyright material. The author and publisher will be glad to rectify any
omissions at the earliest opportunity.

www.orionbooks.co.uk

For Elly and Polly – two very good reasons not to risk my life on the basis of the advice in some dumb list.

Contents

....

Introduction

....

The premise of this book is simple.

It's an anti-list. The list to end all lists. A slacker's bible.

More specifically, it's a direct response to all those top tens, top hundreds and top thousands that dominate modern life.

It's a book for everyone who's fed up of being told what to do with their time. Everyone who is tired of being made to feel inferior just because they haven't shared the same experiences as overgrown schoolboys and over-privileged critics. Everyone who resents having their TV schedules and bookshelves taken over with gigantic but ultimately meaningless lists. In short, it's for everyone.

There are just too many lists in the world telling us what to do with our time – and not enough time to do it all in. Turn on Channel 4 at any time when they aren't showing *Big Brother* and chances are there will be another list of 50 programmes you absolutely must watch before you shuffle off this mortal coil. Buy any Sunday supplement and you're almost guaranteed to be confronted by To-Do lists outlining every book we have to read, every film we have to watch, every TV programme we have to sit through, every holiday destination we have to visit, every indulgent purchase we have to make, every culinary oddity we have to experience and every drop of culture we have to imbibe if we are to consider ourselves fully alive... before we die. It's exhausting.

The last time I entered 'things to do before you die' into Google, more than 2 million entries came up. People are dictating to us on everything from '101 Things to Buy' to '300 Beers to Try' to '50 Things to do in Keighley before you die' ('Go Down the Pool Water Slide' comes in at number five*).

Life just isn't long enough even to read a fraction of these lists, let alone act on their suggestions. Especially since the majority of them are so ludicrous. Is it really a good idea to touch a tiger? To eat rotting shark? How many of us are actually going to have our lives enriched by rolling down a hillside in a plastic bubble?

And that's before we've got to the strange obsession in all these guides about getting up close and personal with aquatic life that would far rather be left alone.

With all entries based on real suggestions from other list books and websites, *Sod That!* will assure its readers that they don't need to feel spiritually inferior just because they haven't gone to all the money and effort of getting to, say, Easter Island. Rampant consumer tourism isn't a moral absolute. But it is bad for the environment. How many people can afford to go to Machu Picchu, after all? Imagine the damage that would

---

* *'Play netball' comes in at number 40.*

be done if everyone did fly all the way to Peru and tramp their way through delicate rainforests to get there.

This book is a rallying call for common sense and dignified indolence over hectic, wasteful and morally dubious over-activity. Sometimes staying at home is the best thing to do with your time and *Sod That!* proves it.

Sam Jordison

April

2008

1

Climb Everest

In March 1923, in an interview with the *New York Times*, British mountaineer George Leigh Mallory claimed he wanted to climb Everest simply 'because it's there'. This statement sounds good only up until the point you actually think about it. Proper consideration reveals that it's a completely ridiculous reason to give for anything. Imagine what you'd think if someone said the same thing about smearing himself in dog poo, for instance.

Tragically, Mallory rather reinforced this argument by dying on the mountain one year later. His sad demise only spurred more people on to 'conquer' the mountain and in recent years it's been opened up to just about anyone with enough money to join an expedition there.

So it is that when someone you know – or your family knows – assays a climb of Everest, their efforts are all you'll hear about for six months: the expense; the having to stump up sponsorship money; the worry (the lots of worry); and then, when (if) he/she returns frostbitten and triumphant, the staggering achievement.

In reality, climbing Everest is about as sensible and safe as running across the traffic on a motorway. But would your parents-in-law put that in their yearly round robin letter? 'X's partner Y [that's you] got incredibly lean after much preparation in the pub and made it across the M25 at Reigate... and back! Of course we are all incredibly proud of his achievement. He did burst his spleen and have his femur cracked in two on the return sprint but is luckily still alive. Pictures on Flickr!'

Just consider: more than 200 people have died attempting the ascent of Everest and thousands have had to be airlifted out of danger – many of them crippled or otherwise permanently injured. Conditions are so difficult that most bodies are left where they fall when people die. Frozen corpses line the major routes up as ghoulish reminders to all other climbers of just how foolish they are.

Every team that climbs Everest leaves an average of 500 kg of rubbish behind, which then freezes onto the side of the great mountain for eternity, ice-preserved woolly mammoth style. Climbers have reported finding medical waste and bloody syringes on the route up and it's said that it's impossible to dig anywhere near the main routes without encountering some kind of trash or frozen human excrement. No longer serene or mysterious, the mountain has become the highest junkyard in the world.

USELESS TRIVIA

▶ Mount Everest is the world's biggest mountain at *c.*29,000 feet.

▶ Permits to climb the mountain cost $25,000.

▶ A guide costs a further $25,000.

▶ Food, fuel and oxygen supplies and tents: a minimum of $40,000.

▶ Helicopter evacuation: $5,000.

▶ On one particularly bad day, 11 May 1996, eight people died trying to get down from Mount Everest.

2

Learn and Perform
the *Kama Sutra*

....

Why are we so in thrall to the notion that bodily contortion
is erotic?

Why have we let goaty New Age gurus convince us that if
we aren't prepared to get more bent up with our lover than
during a game of Twister with a giant centipede, we are
somehow inadequate and boring?

Why would we ever give in to the authority of the attributed
author of the book: 'Nandi', the sacred bull and doorkeeper to
Shiva? Why should we allow our sexual lives to be directed by
a volume that advises: 'if the bone of a peacock or of a hyena
be covered with gold, and tied on the right hand, it makes a
man lovely in the eyes of other people'?

What would actually happen if a man were to take seriously
the book's instruction to rub into his lingam* the 'remains
of a kite who has died a natural death, ground into powder,
and mixed with cowach and honey'? Would it really make

_____

* Penis.

a woman 'subject to his will'? Or would it actually be a bit smelly and off-putting?

Finally, just in case there are any chaps out there still thinking that they might like to follow some of the book's teachings, just study its advice about how best to increase the size of your lingam: 'Rub it with the bristles of certain insects that live in trees, and then, after rubbing it for ten nights with oils... again rub it with the bristles as before. By continuing to do this a swelling will be gradually produced in the lingam... then lie on a cot, and cause his [your] lingam to hang down through a hole in the cot.'

Let's face it. We all just bought the book in the hope that there might be some dirty pictures.* It would be mad to actually put most of its suggestions into practice.

---

* Another sore disappointment, if my edition is anything to go by.

3

Trace Your Family Tree

....

Do the names on those absurdly intricate diagrams mean anything to you at all? Is it really interesting to learn that your great-great-great grandfather worked in a shop? Or that your great-great-great-aunt married someone called Eustace and died in 1823? Do you really need to spend years of your life uncovering this information?

If you are subject to this unfortunate compulsion, then before embarking on the necessarily long and tedious trawls through public records offices it's perhaps worth considering the fact that the entire enterprise of building family trees is based on an almost certainly false premise: that all your relatives have been faithful to their partners.

If you come from a normal family, I'm guessing that in all probability your true line can be traced back no further than your great-grandmother's milkman in the 1920s. Of course, if none of *your* ancestors ever had an affair and you really can trace your genetic line back to Adam, I'm wrong. In that case your family tree research is merely boring.

► American writer Christopher Andersen claims in his book *After Diana* that Prince Harry used to be keen to take a DNA test, but the Queen forbade it. Unless the surprisingly broad-shouldered royal does take the test, his true paternity will remain a mystery, although Andersen also says that the Princess of Hearts met her lover James Hewitt as early as 1981 (not 1984, as the pair later claimed) and that the carrot-topped Major who bears an uncanny resemblance to Harry could indeed be the goofy young prince's father... All of which goes to show that even the most closely and publicly monitored family trees are potentially dubious.

4

Go Parachuting

In a sense, I have a suspicion that there's no point writing this entry. If you're the kind of person who thinks that it's a good idea to spend a fortune in order to throw yourself at the hard ground from a great height, protecting yourself from impact only with a sheet attached to your body by strings, reason and logic probably won't penetrate. If, meanwhile, you're going on a 'jump' (wouldn't it be more accurate to call it a 'fall'?) for charity, I certainly don't want to stop you. No, wait. Scrub that last statement. I do actually want to stop you. It's a stupid thing to do. Why not have a nice peaceful sleep-in for charity instead?

Some will try to tell you that parachuting is a life-enhancing experience and that, should you survive, it will give you a new perspective on the rest of your life. Don't listen to them. You don't need to risk death by splatterdom to realise what an elementary knowledge of gravity can already tell you: you're better off staying on the ground.

The main reason not to go parachuting, however, is that – unless you want to go to all the trouble, expense and risk of properly training to do a solo 'jump' – the only way you can get to fall out of the sky is attached to a qualified instructor. By the buttocks. That's right. You're tied around the middle to a complete stranger. Generally, a big hearty man whose nature can be easily summarised in the fact that he tumbles out of planes for a living.

For practical reasons, you become attached to your new friend on the ground, have to stay together for 30–40 excruciating minutes as your tiny plane makes its perilous way into the skies. Then, you spend 30 awful seconds battling G-forces as you plummet downwards, before your parachute opens and you start spinning round hopelessly, desperately trying not to gush sick up into your companion's face. Finally, you hit the ground and (if you're lucky enough to survive) spend the rest of the day with a splitting gravity-induced headache and a very embarrassed feeling – sadly with none of the fun memories or lovebites that usually accompany these pains.

5

Join a Book Club

....

Book clubs are one of the biggest cultural phenomena of the new millennium. Encouraged by Oprah Winfrey and Richard and Judy, they've sprung up in pubs and sitting rooms around the world faster than mould in a damp bathroom. A 2006 TUC survey even discovered that 91% of employees in Britain would want to join a club if they had the opportunity.

But why go to all that trouble, travel all that way and bake all those cakes just to learn that your friends or colleagues are as wrong about books as they are about everything else?

6

Go to Watch a Formula One Race in Monaco

....

VROOOM! Squeal! VROOOOOOMM!

'Did you see who that was?'

VROOOM

'What?'

'Did you see who that was?'

'What?'

'I said, did you...'

VROOOM! Squeal! VROOOOOOMM!

'I can't hear you. It's too noisy.'

'DID YOU SEE WHO THAT WAS?'

'No.'

'Who?'

'What?'

VROOOM! Squeal! VROOOOOOMM!

'WHO WAS IT?'

'I already told you I don't know.'

VROOOM! Squeal! VROOOOOOMM!

'What?'

'What?'

'I said – oh fuck it. Do you want a beer?'

'What?'

'Beer?'

You make a drinking motion. Your companion understands. You go and get two beers. They cost you £12. And you can't taste them anyway because of the disgusting smell of petrol that hangs in the air. You still can't make out what's happening on the track either. Your ears are hurting. Later, a man in a Ferrari fleece will force you to engage in a conversation about gearboxes. Then you'll lose all your money in the casino. A fitting punishment for taking part in an activity that Jeremy Clarkson approves of.

USELESS TRIVIA

▶ As well as defying most of the normal laws of the universe by being both dangerous and boring at the same time, Formula One races should possibly be avoided on ethical grounds too. The cars burn through a litre of high-octane fuel every kilometre they travel. Even more is used up in jetting the cars and their support teams around the world, and testing the infernal machines in wind tunnels.

Don't let this make you think that the sport is bad for the environment, however! Norbert Haug, head of Mercedes-Benz Motorsport, which provides the engines for McLaren, has shown his critics short shrift, defending the sport on the grounds that millions of people around the world watch Formula One races on television and are thus prevented from using their cars while the race is underway. So there you go.

7

Walk on Fire

....

'Become the Phoenix,' advise the New Age gurus. 'Fire-walk! Experience burning ambition! Heat up your soul!'

The shortest sponsored walk you can do, the 100-foot dash over red-hot coals, is sold to us as an involved spiritual journey. It is, say its promoters, visible proof of how the spiritual can overrule the temporal plane. An ego-nourishing way of turning fear into power.

As well as rattling off sub-yoga dialogue, practitioners are able to produce some impressive religious bona fides. The interestingly named !Kung people have practised fire-walking for as long as they have been in existence. Hindus have done it for thousands of years in their Thimithi festival. Management consultants and highly motivated middle managers have been at it in team building exercises since the early 1970s.

Fire-walking is, we are told, the ultimate test of mind over matter.

In reality, of course, it's a simple case of basic physics outweighing human idiocy. Next time a fire-walker presents you with a mystical explanation of why the heat does not touch their feet, and tries to tell you it's all a case of 'pointing your mind in the right direction', ask them to stand on hot metal plates for a few seconds. The effect will be very different. Charcoal, you see, is chosen for fire-walking because of its poor thermal conductivity. Our bodies are easily able to transfer the heat away in the time the foot spends in contact with the hot stuff. And, in fact, it doesn't even touch that much of it because of the rough surface area of the coal. The process is actually no more remarkable than our ability to put our hands into a hot oven without getting burned – something most people do every day, without demanding sponsorship money.

That's not to say, however, that fire-walking isn't a dumb thing to do. There's still a chance that shards of hot coals might get wedged in your little tootsies, and if the fire has been prepared badly or the walk is timed wrong, the results can be searingly painful. Just don't blame the failure of your mind to create a 'protective shield', a loss of willpower or the malign will of the gods. Blame yourself for doing it in the first place.

USELESS TRIVIA

▸ In 2002, 20 managers of the KFC fast food chain in Australia had to be treated for burns when their team-building fire-walking exercise (presumably an attempt to prove they weren't chicken*) went wrong.

▸ Meanwhile, a 2004 attempt to break the fire-walking world record – and incidentally raise some money for charity – in Dunedin, New Zealand, collapsed into chaos when 28 people suffered serious burns

---

* Sorry.

and 11 had to be rushed to hospital. Their medical bills amounted to far more than the £350 they raised in the first place. Just to rub salt into their blisters and burns, a spokeswoman from the *Guinness Book of Records* then informed the organisers that the fire-walking record is based on distance, not the number of people taking part.

8

Sleep Outside, Under the Stars

....

On paper, camping out in full view of the glories of the night sky sounds wonderful. There you are, snug by a roaring fire, your true love beside you, under the dark roof of heaven, all the little stars winking down at you. Just you! What a glorious mind-expanding experience.

In reality, you're freezing cold, the ground is uncomfortably hard, you feel rotten after eating half-cooked, flame-blackened burgers and then you get soaked by the picturesque dew. It probably rains too. The only thing you really learn is why mankind invented beds and houses in the first place.

9

Buy a Star

....

Naming a star with the International Star Registry, we are told, couldn't be easier. You send in just over $50 with the name you want and they send you back a beautiful parchment with the name of the star that they have registered for you, its co-ordinates and a star chart with the location of your particular astral body circled in red. The company even throw in a letter of congratulations and a booklet on astronomy written by a professional astronomer. Give them another $100 and they'll frame your star chart and give you a wallet.

The best thing is that you can call your little piece of heaven whatever you want. Nicole Kidman got one and called it 'Forever Tom', for instance. Winona Ryder bought one for her then-squeeze Johnny Depp. Two stars have been named after Princess Diana. Unsurprisingly, more than a million have been sold since the International Star Registry started trading in 1979.

There is a small problem, however, aside from the obvious cringe factor. The star names recorded by the International Star Registry are not recognised by any professional astronomical body. So, the stars aren't actually named after you or your loved ones after all. All the ISR (and several similar companies) actually do is register them in a big book.

The International Astronomical Union is the only scientific body authorised to name astronomical bodies and they don't sell them. They say: 'Some commercial enterprises purport to offer such services for a fee. However, such "names" have no formal or official validity whatever: A few bright stars have ancient, traditional Arabic names, but otherwise stars have just catalogue numbers and positions on the sky... Thus, like true love and many other of the best things in human life, the beauty of the night sky is not for sale, but is free for all to enjoy.'

10

Learn How to Do Origami

Origami is the science of making silly animal shapes out of one piece of paper. Or, depending on your point of view, the Japanese art of paper folding. Figures of incredible complexity can be made out of this single sheet and it requires immense skill to make many of the more complicated patterns. But surely, with two pieces you could make even better ones. How about three? Better still, what about using wood and glue and all the other materials man has at his disposal and actually making something durable and useful?

11

Go to the Opera or the Theatre

....

Perhaps it's taking things a bit far to jettison 500 years of what is commonly regarded as the pinnacle of European artistic achievement. But we shouldn't let that stop us. Not least because all the old jokes are true: the opera starts at six o'clock, you sit there for three hours, look at your watch and it's 6.20; the guy gets stabbed in the back and instead of dying he sings…

Going to the opera is like getting drunk – it is a sin that carries its own punishment with it.

Meanwhile, the only thing that the theatre can do that television can't do far better is sit you down next to a middle-aged academic on a mission to prove how clever he is by laughing in your ear at all of Shakespeare's unfunny jokes. Or a sixth-former who, away from parental supervision for just about the first time, has filled his teenage guts with beer before the show and now needs to chunder them up all over you.

12

Swim With Dolphins

....

Swimming with dolphins is one of the world's fastest growing tourist activities and one of its most profitable, so much so that each dolphin in captivity, unbeknown to the animal, is now worth more than £100,000.

The appeal is obvious. Our no-legged friends are very cute; they look like they're smiling all the time; they can do clever tricks with balls, while endless New Age balls about ESP and how they can talk to you through sonar has been ascribed to them. 'Watching their exquisite movements and listening to a symphony of sound you feel part of their magical world,' claim the holiday websites, and who wouldn't want that? Especially since getting in the water with the animals is promoted as such a beneficial therapeutic activity, and the BBC has shown a film of Olympic medallist Sharron Davies frolicking with the laughing sea mammals.

Fun as it may be for us, however, it's a reasonable assumption that not every dolphin will welcome having their busy, tiring day interrupted by boatloads of screaming tourists, eager to jostle around them in the water, grab hold of their dorsal fin, and ram a camera in their faces.

Worse yet, dolphins quickly become acclimatised to being fed and distracted by humans. They become friendly and start getting too near to boats. They then get caught up in ropes, bashed by sterns and ripped apart by propellers.

Here's another little secret. Dolphins aren't smiling at you: they're opening their mouths. It's not the same thing. It certainly doesn't mean that they enjoy being tampered with all day long for the entertainment of tourists. It doesn't mean that they're delighted to meet Sharron Davies. Look at a picture of a dead dolphin. Looks like it's smiling too, doesn't it?

USELESS TRIVIA

► The Whale and Dolphin Conservation Society (WDCS) claims there is no evidence that swimming with dolphins helps people with physical or learning difficulties.

► A report by the same organisation says that dolphins suffer severe stress when they encounter people, they frequently attack swimmers and they can transmit brucellosis to us. Brucellosis is an infectious disease that can lead to spontaneous abortion in pregnant women. Don't worry, however: we get the animals back. We give dolphins chickenpox – against which they have no immunity whatsoever.

13

Dive With Sharks

....

Combines nearly all of the disadvantages of swimming with dolphins with huge sharp teeth and a hard, cold-blooded lust. And that's just the tour companies trying to persuade you to take part in this crazy activity.

14

Eat Hákarl:
the World's Weirdest Dish

....

One of the strangest modern tests of manhood is the ability to eat hákarl. This indelicacy is served up during Thorrablot, Iceland's midwinter festival. Its full name is kæstur hákarl – which translated means fermented shark. The shark in question is the Somniosus Microphalus*, an ugly cannibalistic brute generally found haunting the shores of Greenland. It would be bad enough to swim with it. To eat it is sheer folly. The beast is full of uric acid and trimethylamine oxide so if people try to eat it before it's been processed, they puke blood. If they eat it after it's been processed, they just puke.

Preparing the shark for human consumption takes time and patience. First the fish must be gutted and washed in salt water. Then it is buried in coarse gravel, ideally close to the sea and far from the nearest settlement in order to ensure that the rancid smell doesn't upset anyone. Then it's left for up to three months, weighed down by stones, to rot and putrefy.

---

* *Best translated as 'Sleepy Little Penis'.*

After this curing period, the shark is cut into strips and hung out to dry for several more months, during which time a brown crust forms on its surface. Prior to serving, the scabby brown stuff is scraped off and the fish meat is cut into small chunks and dished up with an ice-cold shot of brennivín, a fierce Icelandic spirit that dulls the disgusting sensations the rotting fish flesh creates in the mouth.

Those who have tried hárkal have said that it smells like a cross between strong cleaning products and stale urine. According to internet travel writer Michael Middleton it tastes like: 'the Predator wading into a Care Bears movie and opening fire'. Chef Anthony Bourdain, who encountered hárkal after several seasons sampling food from around the world for his American TV show, described it as 'the single worst, most disgusting and terrible tasting thing' he had ever eaten. Such words shouldn't be taken lightly considering the fact that he once downed a shot of cobra bile. When the famously tough UK chef Gordon Ramsay ate hákarl, he was immediately and violently sick.

There really is no need to eat it.

15

Take Out the One You Love on St Valentine's Day

....

Nothing is really known about the St Valentine whose feast is celebrated on 14 February, although the most popular legend has it that he was beaten to death with clubs some time in the third century AD, during the reign of the second emperor Claudius. Then his head was chopped off and put on a spike.

That fate might seem preferable to forgetting to treat your better half on the year's biggest Hallmark holiday, but why not stay in and thus strike a blow against having the timetable of your life dictated by people hawking pink-toned gifts, against reducing your love to a syrupy gloop of heart-shaped confectionary and against overbooked restaurants? Who knows, you could actually get it on instead of going through all that absurd foreplay, and then go out for a genuinely romantic meal the next day when all the restaurants are quieter.

USELESS TRIVIA

► The American greeting card association estimates that 1 billion Valentine's cards are sent each year, which raises a few interesting questions considering that the country has just over 304 million inhabitants.

Meanwhile, in a neat demonstration of the baleful influence of commercial enterprises in inventing traditions, the people of Sweden were lucky enough not to follow any Valentine's traditions until a consortium of flower sellers launched the concept of All Hearts' Day there in the 1960s. Now the poor Swedes buy more cosmetics and greetings cards for All Hearts' Day than for any other occasion except Mother's Day.

16

Try to Get on TV

Look at the people on TV: Sharon Osbourne, Lawrence Llewelyn-Bowen, Noel Edmonds, Bruce Forsyth, Boris Johnson, Jade Goody, Jeremy Clarkson. Do you really want to be like them? Worse yet, do you want to hang out with them?

17

Learn Another Language

Let's face it – people speak enough bollocks in English anyway. Why waste all that time and effort just so you can listen to even more people talking out of their backsides? And let me tell you from hard-learned experience, there is nothing to be gained from reading Sartre in the original language except more confusion and pain.

18

Drink a Fine Vintage Wine

Can you detect the oaky flavours? Do you think this vintage is redolent of the moist laps of buxom, healthful, country girls? Does the hint of raspberries set your palate alight?

Me neither.

Does it, actually, just taste quite nice and slowly get you pleasantly drunk? And is that anything that a £5 bottle from Oddbins doesn't do? And is it really worth the massive price difference considering the fact that, in the end, you'll wee out both drinks just the same?

USELESS TRIVIA

▶ President Thomas Jefferson is widely regarded as the USA's first wine buff. He is said to have spent $7,500 on wine in his lifetime (around a quarter of a million dollars in today's money) and was particularly fascinated by the flavour of French Bordeaux.

▶ He was also, more pertinently, the country's first wine bore. 'There was, as usual, a dissertation upon wines,' noted John Quincy Adams in his diary after dining with the revolutionary leader in 1807. 'Not very edifying.'

- In 1985, Christopher Forbes (of the Forbes magazine family) acquired what was thought to be a surviving bottle from Jefferson's supply for £105,000. 'It's more fun than the opera glasses Lincoln was holding when he was shot,' he declared, before adding smugly: 'And we have those, too.'

- The bottle took pride of place on a dining table in the presidential memorabilia section of the Forbes museum, where the heat from the spotlights warped the cork, causing it to fall into the bottle and ruin the wine.

19

Eat Brussels Sprouts

Even more astonishing than the fact that hundreds of bloggers have joined forces across the internet to share their thoughts on the five foods they'd like to eat just before they die (when surely they should be more worried about getting a doctor to find a cure double-quick) is the fact that Brussels sprouts featured heavily.

The cabbage's poorer, smaller cousin is, as we are often told, a very good source of many essential vitamins, fibre and something called folate. Sprouts have also been shown to have some very beneficial effects against certain types of cancer and for years nutritionists have been urging us to eat more of them for the good of our health.

Defenders of the sprout proclaim that most of the unpleasant sulphurous smells associated with them come as a result of overcooking. If steamed correctly, they say, sprouts actually have a delicate nutty flavour. This isn't true.

Crucially, moreover, they not only produce farts but taste like them too. I suppose our foody friends do have something of a point; why prolong life if you intend to fill it with the misery of eating sprouts? But is that really how you want your last breath to smell?

20

Make Your Own Bread

....

Ahhh! The feeling of wet dough in your hands. Oh, the wonderful knowledge connecting you with the generations of humans before you who have made their own loaves. Urgh! The horrible taste of it when it comes out of the oven. Ouch! The way it mixes itself into concrete in your guts and drops out of your bowels like a particularly horrible moment in the bombing of Dresden.

21

Ride the World's
Biggest Rollercoaster

It's frightening. It goes too fast. It's unnatural. The seat is uncomfortable. It's undignified. You're upside down at 50 mph for God's sake. Your face goes red. Something bad is happening to your stomach. Something involving figures of eight, severe swift food dislodgement and near unbearable gut-wrenching strain. Someone is sick on you. So you are sick too. Someone else hurts your ears with their screaming. When you get to the end, your legs are wobbly and all of your friends laugh at you for being a wuss.

Then they build a bigger one somewhere else six weeks later.

USELESS TRIVIA

▶ An average of two to three people die every year on rollercoasters in the USA. Less depressingly, a woman from Gloucestershire recently claimed that a rollercoaster ride saved her from a brain tumour. After riding on the Incredible Hulk ride in Florida, Sally Dare experienced terrible headaches and blurred vision. When doctors examined her they discovered that the jolting and shuddering of the ride had dislodged a brain tumour, which they promptly removed. 'I could still be walking around for another year or two, still sort of not knowing,' said Ms Dare. 'So, if it did dislodge while banging about on the rollercoaster and they caught it early then maybe it's a good thing.' But even though this story proves that rollercoasters have their uses in alerting people to nasty things they might have in their brains, it does rather raise the question of whether a bout of shaking and head-rattling vigorous enough to dislodge a tumour is actually a sensible thing to put yourself through...

MORE USELESS TRIVIA

▶ At the time of writing, the world's biggest rollercoaster (going by height) is Kingda Ka: a 456 ft, 128 mph tower of terror in New Jersey. By the time you are reading these words, it will no doubt be different.

22

Go to the North Pole

To many the North Pole represents the extreme of human experience; the literal top of the world. One of the sternest challenges in the eternal battle between man and nature. One of the few places that remain unpolluted by Starbucks or McDonald's.

But if you actually make it there*, you will discover that it's cold, lifeless and there's nothing to see. This experience can be recreated with far less expense and bother by going to Dunfermline. Or listening to the music of Phil Collins.

USELESS TRIVIA

▸ The South Pole is rather like the North Pole. The weather is reported to be equally inclement, with the unpleasant addition that many who get there suffer altitude sickness since it's situated at 3,000 metres above sea level. It's so far from the ocean that the air is drier than it is in the Sahara. So don't go there either.

---

* *Wearing, incidentally, a thermal outfit that firstly looks ridiculous and secondly negates all idea of challenge and actually taking on the icy wilderness on its own terms.*

23

Wear a Kilt

....

You probably don't need to be told that kilts look ridiculous. Nor that they're heavy, itchy and wearing one greatly increases your chances of being mistaken for a minor British royal and victim of inbreeding.

So let's not consider the possibility that anyone should wear this ungainly man-dress because they think it's cool. But even so, the real reasons people still go to the trouble of wrapping themselves up in this ugly tartan dress are equally daft. Even if we leave aside the fact that you can never really know your true genetic make-up, imagining that a kilt links you to your Gaelic ancestry and a traditional Highland way of life is still a big mistake.

The 'traditional ancient dress of the Highlands', you see, was introduced to Scotland by an Englishman in the eighteenth century. This man, Thomas Rawlinson, had noticed that the authentic Highland dress worn by his employees north of the border was 'a cumbrous unwieldy habit' so he got the tailor from the local (English) army regiment to design something more suitable. The tailor came up with the kilt design and the rest is history – but maybe not history as Scottish nationalist kilt-wearers would have it.

USELESS TRIVIA

► Clan tartans are an even later invention than kilts. And yes, once again, they were invented by Englishmen. Tartan was introduced to Scotland in the sixteenth century from Flanders, and the colour and pattern worn by individuals was simply a matter of fashion (if fashion is a word that can ever be applied to tartan). It was enterprising weavers who realised there was considerable commercial advantage in making up differentiated clan tartans in the early nineteenth century.

► Meanwhile, if you're ever unlucky enough to encounter a man wearing a kilt who is also playing the bagpipes, it might also be worth reminding him that up until the nineteenth century, the traditional instrument of the Highlands was the harp.

24

Ride in a Gondola in Venice

....

The observant traveller to the beautiful city of Venice will notice two things relating to gondolas. Firstly that no locals will ever go near them. Secondly that at best the gondoliers treat their passengers with haughty disdain and contemptuous silence.

Of course, that's no way to treat anyone, but gondoliers can be forgiven for looking down on anyone foolish enough to procure their services. They know, for a start, that you get a far better, far more comprehensive and far cheaper view of the city if you catch one of the excellent local waterbuses. They know you wish they were singing, but that they won't do it, no matter how much you try to tip them. They know you're trying to make a cheesy cliché the highlight of your life. They also know you've just paid €100 to float around for half an hour on sewage water. In short, they know you're a sucker.

25

Visit Easter Island

··

There's no denying the strange beauty of the famous statues that stare out to sea from this remote Pacific island. There's also something uniquely compelling in their mystery. Why would anyone go to the trouble of erecting these 600-odd statues, many of them weighing more than 250 tons? How did the islanders ever get them up in the first place? What do they signify?

Far easier to explain is the fact that the civilisation that created these eerie statues soon afterwards tore itself apart. Historians and anthropologists have blamed their disastrous infighting and land pillaging on deforestation and a mysterious local cult of the 'birdman', but the true answer will become immediately clear to anyone who makes the mammoth journey to this remote speck of land: boredom and frustration.

Easter Island is surrounded by more than a million square miles of Pacific Ocean and the nearest populated area is more than 1,200 miles away (the even duller incest-ridden Pitcairn islands). It takes more than five hours by plane to get to the nearest continent and there are only a handful of flights every week. This remoteness is an especial problem since, other than to get drunk and go crazy, there is nothing to do there once you've traipsed around a few of the statues. And let's face it: once you've seen one, you've seen them all.

USELESS TRIVIA

▶ The native Easter islanders used to call their home the *Te pito o te henua*, the 'navel of the world' because it was so isolated. Further evidence of their unhappy state comes in one of their favourite insults, as recorded by European visitors in the nineteenth century: 'the flesh of your mother sticks between my teeth'.

▶ The 'birdman' cult was practised on the island until the 1860s. The 'birdman' was the winner of a competition to collect the first Sooty Tern egg of the season by swimming to the neighbouring islet of Moto Nui. This lucky fellow was given control of the distribution of the island's resources for the next year – and generally doled them out exclusively to his own family and friends, causing misery and starvation for the rest of the islanders.

26

Spend New Year's Eve in Times Square, New York

....

5 p.m. You arrive in Times Square, knowing that had you arrived any later, you wouldn't have got in.

5.02 p.m. You notice how cold it is now that you've stopped walking. You wonder vaguely how you will manage seven hours.

5.04 p.m. Someone makes a bad joke about what an appropriate place Times Square is to spend New Year's Eve.

5.14 p.m. Someone else makes a bad joke about what an appropriate place Times Square is to spend New Year's Eve. [And repeat, every ten minutes, until 1 a.m.]

6 p.m. All the streets around have been closed by the authorities and you have now been effectively barricaded in with half a million other people, and no escape from the giant advertising hoardings intent on selling you things you don't need or want.

6.30 p.m. You are so bored that you start tucking into the alcohol supply that you have had to covertly sneak into the area inside a soft drink bottle.

7 p.m. You discover that you need the toilet. And that there are 500,000 people between you and relief.

8 p.m. You are colder than you have ever been in your life and sobering up rapidly.

9.30 p.m. City sanitation workers start handing out FREE STUFF. There's a mad scramble. When, at the risk of life and limb, you finally manage to grab some of it, you discover that you've got some balloons, some pompoms and an 'Official Times Square Confetti' bag.

10 p.m. The needing-the-toilet thing really isn't funny any more.

10.30 p.m. Music starts blaring from the on-street PA system and you are forced to sing along to mawkish pop anthems with 500,000 people you now really hate.

11.30 p.m. It's still cold. You still need the toilet. You can't wait for the old year to die.

11.58 p.m. You discover that your view of 'The Ball', whose dropping will signify the beginning of the new year, is obscured by half a million people who are trying to take pictures of it on their camera phones. You try to get a picture too, but all you can capture is other people's raised phones.

11.59 p.m. The countdown begins.

12 a.m. The Ball has dropped, an electric sign with the new date on it has lit up. And that's it. Some people are cheering and waving flags, but nothing else has changed.

12.01 a.m. Someone you don't know tries to hug you, causing excruciating pain in your bladder.

12.02 a.m. The whooping people are now starting to really annoy you and you are having dark thoughts about futility, mutability and mortality. Was that it? It seems that nothing has happened except that you have got older.

12.10 a.m. You realise how long it is going to take you to get through the crowd to whichever overpriced hole you are staying in – and how much the taxi driver is going to over-charge you for the privilege.

1 a.m. You still haven't managed to go to the toilet. Plenty of other people have though, and their urine is slicking the streets and forming yellow icicles against the fire hydrants. This is the image that will remain with you, long after the rest has faded into a still-painful, but thankfully blurred and half-forgotten memory.

USELESS TRIVIA ....

► The tradition of the ball drop from One Times Square dates back to 1907. In 2007, to celebrate its centenary, a new ball was created. According to the official New York tourism website, 'The Ball' is actually a geodesic sphere. It's more than six feet in diameter, weighs over 1,000 pounds, is covered with hundreds of Waterford crystal triangles, is lit by more than 9,000 ultra-high-tech LED bulbs, around100 high-intensity strobes and contains 90 rotating pyramid mirrors. It looks shit.

27

Spend New Year's Eve in Edinburgh

....

Combines most of the problems of New Year's Eve in New York with the added risk of someone in a kilt* blasting bagpipe music at you.

---

* *See entry 23 to understand this person's foolishness.*

28

Climb an Active Volcano

On a good day the view at the top of a volcano is awesome. The very bowels of the earth boil and bubble in that great crater. In that vast, glowing hollow you feel like you are watching the angry orange indigestion of the gods. Thunderous eruptions belch up from the depths, with great burpings of red-hot magma spewing over the sides. It's an amazing thing to see and almost worth the climb and risk. Except that: on a bad day, you're toast.

USELESS TRIVIA

▶ Lava in volcanoes can reach temperatures of 1,250°C. The first recorded volcano spotter in history was the Roman naturalist Pliny the Elder. His nephew Pliny the Younger described his trip across the sea to see the exploding Mount Vesuvius in AD 79 thus: 'He steered his course direct to the point of danger, and with so much calmness and presence of mind as to be able to make and dictate his observations upon the motion and all the phenomena of that dreadful scene.' Then, unsurprisingly, the elder Pliny was killed. His body was found two days later under a pile of ashes.

29

Go Ski-ing

There's nothing new to jokes about Fotherington-Thomases and their ghastly children mashing up the delicate ecosystems of mountain slopes by careering down them in outfits worth enough money to keep several small towns in food for a year. Most people will also have heard all the horror stories about shin bones snapping like lolly sticks, elbows popping out from under your skin and having to eat fondue. But it's still worth pointing out the sheer awfulness of ski-ing because more than 1 million Britons every year continue to insist on lining themselves up for this odds-on death-slide entry to the casualty wards.

Actually carting yourself off to a cold mountainside and queuing for lifts surrounded by impatient and unpleasant snow-tourists seems especially foolish since the whole experience is so easily recreated in the comfort of your own home. OK, unless you import a sunbed and sit facing it all week while wearing a mask you won't be able to accurately render the post-ski barn owl look. Your chances of being hit on the back of the head by a stoned teenage snowborder are also considerably reduced if you do choose to remain on your sofa. All the same, most of the other sensations of the ski-ing holiday are easily rendered: simply apply a trouser press to your legs for a week* and then jump off the top of a ladder to recreate the physical sensations. Invite an annoying five-year-old (preferably from Germany or Scandinavia) to come and run rings around you so you can live through all those emotions of inadequacy. Finally, in order to conjure up the joyless atmosphere of après-ski, retire to bed at 8 p.m. because you're too tired to do anything else, having pre-requested that your neighbours keep you awake all night with drunken shouting.

USELESS TRIVIA

▶ According to legend, if you drink cold water with your fondue, the melted cheese recongeals into a hard ball in your stomach, providing digestion problems rivalled only by eating car tyres**.

---

* *And if that seems like a ridiculous idea to you, just compare it to putting on salopettes (an item of clothing that manages to combine all the worst qualities of dungarees and nappies), clamping your feet into plastic boots, strapping sticks to those, gathering up two spiked poles to help you steer and then leaping off the side of an icy mountain.*

** *The author wishes to note that if he could have written a separate entry about the horrors of communally eating molten cheese, he would. Surprisingly, however, he was unable to find one list that recommended it and so he has been forced to resort to the devious means employed above to ensure its inclusion in this volume.*

30

Go Dirtboarding

··

Just like ski-ing, snowboarding could also be described as a foolish activity. Strapping yourself to a single plank of wood and throwing yourself off a mountainside does run counter to most of our evolutionary instincts after all. Further proof of the folly of this activity is demonstrated by the fact that between 1998 and 2004 nearly 40,000 snowboarding injuries were treated in France alone.

But snowboarding has nothing on dirtboarding since it at least has the virtue of being carried out on a lovely soft cushion of the white stuff. Dirtboarding, as the name implies, does away with such fripperies. If you should tumble from your oversized skateboard now, no powdery pillow protects you. At best you can hope for mud – and the mentality of those that take part in the activity is neatly summed up by the fact that they call such an accident: 'chewing hill'.

One website for this relatively new sport explains that it is best described as 'riding a bike but with no hands' – down a mountain. The idea is to strap yourself to a piece of fibreboard with over-inflated pram-style wheels and point yourself straight down the side of a steep slope. Its advocates tend to be decorated in Celtic tattoos, boast that they can attain speeds of up to 50 mph, and point out the advantage that 'dirt doesn't melt'. They also note that the best practitioners in their field demonstrate 'sick styling'. The device that is used to stop the board, meanwhile, is known appositely as 'the dead man's brake'.

If you do attempt a descent and you do (inevitably) go for a burton, the probability of there being a far more skilful crowd of teenagers on hand to laugh at you is greater than one. You will also – one way or another – ruin your trousers.

31

Throw a Dart in a Map and Travel Where it Lands

In the abstract this oft repeated idea promises all the excitement of the unknown. What adventures you might have on your journey to absolutely anywhere!

In reality, it's that 'anywhere' that causes the problem. What if the dart lands in the middle of the Atlantic? Or right next to your house? To throw it again is to admit that you aren't leaving your journey to chance at all. To actually journey somewhere really crap just because a dart told you to do so is the height of idiocy.

If you aim the dart, you're cheating. If you don't aim, it might not even hit the map at all and might well cause an accident. Why not just choose to go somewhere you think you might enjoy instead? And then put your darts to their proper use: fending off Jehovah's Witnesses, Mormons and door-to-door salesmen from the comfort of an upstairs room.

32

Stand on the
International Date Line

....

'Whoo whoo! Look at me! I've got my right foot in today and my left foot in yesterday! No no no! Wait! Actually, I've got my left foot in today and my right in tomorrow!'

There is a pause.

Then: 'So that's it, I guess.'

Not much of a thrill really, considering how difficult it is to get to the only land area cartographers recognise as being crossed by the line: the otherwise slightly dull island of Kiribati in the middle of the Pacific Ocean.

USELESS TRIVIA..

▸ Although some map-makers still draw the date line across Kiribati, the island republic itself has moved it to its east. Previously, businesses and government offices on opposite sides of the line could only communicate on the four days when they experienced weekdays simultaneously.

33

Stay in a
Five Star Hotel

....

Saving up to stay in a five star hotel isn't the exquisite self-indulgent treat we are led to believe it might be. Unless you're avid to have sex in a really expensive location*, the best you're going to hope for is a good night's sleep; in which case a good stiff drink is far less hassle and far less likely to come equipped with gold frills. Plus, when you retire to your own room in your own house – unlike in a hotel – you can 100% guarantee that no one has died in the bed before you arrived, or indeed spent the previous night sticking foreign objects into their orifices.

---

* *In which case, a few hours in an antigravity machine will give you a far more interesting return for your money.*

34

Chase a Tornado

....

Only modern man has taken it into his head to chase tornadoes. Our ancestors knew exactly the right response to a life-threatening whirlwind: get the fuck away from it.

To do otherwise is perverse and wrong. Sure, you might get a vaguely interesting film of a few things flying through the air and other people's lives and property being destroyed, but unless you have a car that you're certain can go faster than 250 mph off-road that you can be in when the storm hits, you might come to regret your voyeuristic hobby.

Tornadoes can overturn cars after all. They can also rain down hailstones as big as your head. And sometimes cows. (That's cows flying through the air rather than really big hailstones, which sounds quite funny until you consider the prospect of one of them moving towards you at speed – and the painful landing the poor creature faces.) They rip the roofs off houses. They tear down power lines and start huge fires. They blast the landscape with lightning. They will not stop for you.

▸ Storm-chasing is a high-risk hobby and strict safety precautions have to be followed in order to minimise the danger. Naturally, these measures are frequently ignored and have been evermore frequently since the 1989 film *Twister* encouraged thousands to take up the hobby. These reckless newbies are described as 'yahoos' by more experienced storm chasers. 'These are the people,' fulminates veteran Roger Edwards on his website 'who have decided that chasing is "kewl dude". without taking the time to learn how to do it right.' 'Yahoos' have been blamed for knocking other vehicles off the road in their hurry to get to a tornado scene, blocking out the radio signals of other chasers, ignoring police roadblocks, mashing up private land with their four-wheel drives and (bizarrely) stealing food from the offices of weather forecasters. The most infamous 'yahoo' incident occurred in 1999 when a tornado destroyed a house in Oklahoma City and its injured occupants crawled out from under it to be greeted by the sight of a vehicle stopping in their driveway. Instead of helping the battered and dazed former homeowners, however, the people in the car got out and started shooting a video of the scene before speeding off after the storm again, running over a dog in the process.

35

Drink a Nice Cup of
Kopi Luwak, Animal Coffee

....

Kopi Luwak, we are told, is the world's finest coffee. It's made from coffee beans that have been eaten by and passed through the digestive tract of the Asian Palm Civet and hand-collected from the rainforest floor on the islands of Sumatra, Java and Sulawesi in the Indonesian archipelago.

Or, translated, it's jungle weasel turds.

At least, that's the theory. In fact, some plantation owners have recently been discovered to be force-feeding beans to civets in cages, which is a good reason for free-range supporters to give this exciting beverage a miss.

The drink is supposed to be 'uniquely smooth', with (perhaps unsurprisingly) 'a strong flavour and aroma'. The department store Peter Jones in London's Sloane Square also sold the coffee to discerning punters for a short period for £50 a cup and it's been alleged that its regular drinkers include Damien Hirst. In a sense, then, it's the ultimate microcosm of capitalism: the system whose sole intent is to sell shit to fools at the highest possible price.

▸ It's feared that civets help pass on Sars. In China thousands have already been exterminated. Sars has a 15% mortality rate and kills you by stopping you breathing and boiling your blood.

36

Get into the
Guinness Book of Records

....

The *Guinness Book of Records* has been a staple of Christmas stockings for decades*, which seems to have given rather too many people the idea that they might like to be included within its garish pages – and rather too many 'To-do' list manufacturers the idea that that's something to aim for.

The primary problem with this desire is that the majority of the good records are out of the reach of most of us mortals. No matter what your self-help book says, you can't do anything and everything. You won't become the world's fastest sprinter unless you're extremely talented, train for years and probably take dangerous and illegal performance-enhancing drugs. You won't be able to add up bigger sums than whichever weird kid from the Midwest holds the record. There can only be one World's Tallest Man (see below) and if you don't have the right genetic make-up, you're never going to be able to beat him.

The net result of all that is that the only records left up

-----

* *Thereby neatly earning itself a world record as the bestselling copyrighted book series of all time.*

for grabs are the frankly ridiculous ones. Do you really want to be remembered for not cutting your fingernails? (Besides, you'll never beat the current world record holder, Sridhar Chillal, who spent more than 20 years bringing up his total nail length on a single hand to 20ft 2.25in).

There are a few that seem eminently beatable: most T-shirts worn at one time (155 by Matt McAllister of California); speed cream-cracker-eating (Ambrose Mendy, UK, three crackers in 49.15 seconds – easy!); largest collection of personal belly-button fluff (currently held by Graham Barker, Australia*). But holding such titles does not prove that you are the best at something. It simply proves that you are the biggest idiot.

USELESS TRIVIA

▸ At the time of writing, the world's tallest living man is 37-year-old Ukranian Leonid Stadnyk who stands at an impressive 2.57 m. The fact that he can change light bulbs from a seating position is scant compensation for the accompanying problems caused by his huge size and failing health. Friends say he now needs to hold on to the limbs of trees or the side of houses to get around.

Ironically enough, he was small at school and his nickname was 'titch'. He started an extraordinary growth spurt aged 14 when surgery on a benign brain tumour had an unusual side effect on his pituitary gland, sending his growth hormones into overdrive. He now wears size 27 shoes, calls his height 'God's biggest punishment for me' and refuses to look in a mirror.

----

* Graham has been collecting 'navel lint' since 1984. He keeps it in large glass jars. He estimates that he accumulates 3.03 mg of the fluff each day.

....

▸ Following the publication of a record for the world's heaviest cat, hundreds of cat owners began to overfeed their pets to get them into the book instead. The entry was swiftly removed to protect our feline friends.

37

Own a
Pointless Collection

....

Why? What's the point?

38

Be Present When Your Country Wins the World Cup

All list books should be strictly forbidden from including this suggestion in future, on the grounds that it's infinitely cruel to British people to suggest that they should judge the relative fulfilment of their lives on such an unlikely eventuality. It's bad enough when you're English, while there's more chance of Margaret Thatcher winning the next London Marathon and donating all her sponsorship to a coal miner's benevolent fund than there is of us ever seeing a representative of Scotland, Wales or Northern Ireland lift that much coveted trophy.

But really, it doesn't matter anyway.

It's an absurd idea to think that the achievements of a bunch of overpaid soccer stars in any way relate to you or your life. The average millionaire sportsman cares far less about your existence than the toxic hair gel he smears over his carefully dyed and preened barnet. He's been locked away from the reality of everyday life in a football academy since the age of 11 and he earns more in a week than most of us earn in a lifetime. He's capable of saying things like 'we lost because we didn't win' in all sincerity. He probably doesn't even know how to buy a bus ticket. Nothing he does bears any relation to any of the rest of us. So cease to worry about him, just like he will never worry about you.

39

Read *Ulysses*

....

If you do, as we're all urged, take up James Joyce's overlong magnum opus, it is guaranteed to clog up your all too short life. Banned, criticised and suppressed on moral grounds when it first came out, it thereby became far more famous and far more durable than it would ever have been otherwise. Had it been published openly originally, the book would in all probability have been ignored, or at least gained wider recognition for the pretentious nonsense it is. The lives of generations of English Literature undergraduates the world over would have been considerably eased as a result.

Many readers might experience a strange feeling of guilt at thus disregarding a book that has come to be considered as such an important part of the mythical literary canon. Wading through *Ulysses* is often regarded as a kind of coming of age. You have to get through it to prove your worth to those invisible cultural arbiters who we imagine sit in judgement of us all. You have to know what happened to Leopold Bloom and Stephen Dedalus in Dublin on 16 June 1904, even though the answer is, basically, nothing.

The other thing to remember about trying to prove your bookish credentials by knowing about *Ulysses* is that no one who actually possesses a wide knowledge of literature will believe you if you try to convince them you've read every word. They – having attempted to grind through it themselves – will understand what a thankless task it is.

OK, there are some fine qualities to the book. There's some magnificent wordplay, some world-beating writing and top-class rudery. But a few clever turns of phrase and a couple of pervy passages don't make up for the fact that if you want to understand even half of it you have to lug a dictionary-sized user's guide around with it – unappealing when the book alone already weighs more than a small child.

The only passages that do make sense are the rude ones. So just do what everyone else does and cut straight to them. Skip the rest. Especially skip the 150-odd pages of punctuation-bereft prose that starts: 'Deshil Holles Eamus. Deshil Holles Eamus. Deshil Holles Eamus' and ends 'anyway I wish hed sleep in some bed by himself with his cold feet on me give us room even to let a fart God or do the least thing better yes hold them like that a bit on my side piano quietly sweeeee theres that train far away pianissimo eeeee one more song.'

Everything you need to know about this section is neatly contained in the word 'nonsense'.

There is at least one good thing to be said about *Ulysses*, however. It does at least also have the distinct advantage of not being *Finnegans Wake*. Now that's a book you should die before reading.

USELESS TRIVIA

- On *Ulysses'* first release the *Sporting Times* declared that the book: 'appears to have been written by a perverted lunatic.' Paper of record the *New York Times* opined: 'The average intelligent reader will glean little or nothing from it – even from careful perusal, one might properly say study, of it – save bewilderment and a sense of disgust.' The popular critic 'Aramis', meanwhile, correctly pointed out that: 'Two thirds of it is incomprehensible.'

MORE USELESS TRIVIA

- A 2007 poll commissioned by teletext discovered that 28% of Britons confessed to being unable to finish *Ulysses*, making it the third most unread book in the country following DBC Pierre's *Vernon God Little* and *Harry Potter and the Goblet of Fire*.

40

Run a Marathon

....

Until you think about it too hard, the story of the first marathon is romantic and noble. There's brave Pheidippides, flinging down his shield after the bloody battle of Marathon, already exhausted as he sets out on the long, hard road to Athens where the gathered assembly wait in fear to hear his news. Will they be saved or are they doomed to live under the yoke of their enemies the Persians? Their answer comes when Pheidippides bursts onto the scene just under 26 miles later and cries out: 'We have won!' Then, immediately, he dies at their feet, exhausted by his exertions.

The problem comes when you start to consider the logistics of this famous run. For instance, if Pheidippides was really the sharp, heroic fellow his champions would have us believe, why did he not ride a horse? Surely that would have got the message to the Athenians faster? Plus, if his side had already won the battle, what was the big hurry? The assembly weren't in danger. They could have waited and poor old Pheidippides could simply have re-entered the city in triumph with the rest of the soldiers.

Pretty quickly, the story stops making sense, so it comes as no surprise to learn that there are no real historical sources to back it up. The prosaic truth is that the legend mainly seems to be the invention of over-imaginative Victorians*. If only they realised that Pheidippides would have been better off taking a horse, we'd have been saved a hundred years of misery. The television viewers of the world would also have been spared harrowing footage of Paula Radcliffe emptying her bowels on camera; of zany radio presenters dressed up in bear suits for 'charidee'; and of numerous otherwise healthy people expiring in front of them. Also we would all have been able to avoid the obligation of giving £10 sponsorship to that annoying man from accounts for doing something most of us could do far better – and with far less heartache all round – on a bike.

---

* *Especially the poet Robert Browning who wrote a really very bad mini-epic on Pheidippides' mad dash, entitled simply Pheidippides. Sample lines:*

I stood
Quivering,—the limbs of me fretting as fire frets, an inch from dry wood:
'Persia has come, Athens asks aid, and still they debate?
Thunder, thou Zeus! Athene, are Spartans a quarry beyond
Swing of thy spear? Phoibos and Artemis, clang them "Ye must"!'

The other 100-odd lines are equally painful.

41

Go on a Diet

....

The main reason not to go on a diet is that it turns you into a crashing bore. Your latest food regime might make you obsess about how many calories you've consumed and how many pounds you've shed, but no one else is the remotest bit interested.

There are also important practical considerations. The key to sustained weight loss is to eat moderate amounts of healthy food and get plenty of exercise as a matter of course – not to alter your normal behaviour for a short period of time. The whole idea of dieting is counterproductive. A brief calorie holiday involving lots of vomit-flavoured shakes may help you to shed a few pounds in the short term, but in the long term it's useless since restricting your food intake also improves your body's ability to store fat. Small wonder that 95% of slimmers are said to regain their weight within five years.

But even though they're pointless, don't expect to stop hearing about new diets any time soon. The diet industry is worth an estimated $100 billion in the US alone (more than the combined value of their government's budget for health, education and welfare). What's more, diets provide good copy. Reading that moderation and exercise are the best ways to lose weight is as boring as it is depressing, which is why no more will be said on the subject here. Instead, like every other Sunday supplement, let's cut straight to the whacked-out diet plans.

Although nutrition and calories are modern concepts, diets have been with us for centuries. One of the first known food faddists was Melania the Younger, an early Christian saint who recommended self-starvation in the fifth century AD as a good way of getting close to Jesus. The folly of following her advice is perhaps best demonstrated by the fact that she also spent a large portion of her life crammed into a box deliberately designed to be too small to accommodate her.

Just over 500 years later, in AD 1087, William the Conqueror is said to have restricted himself to a liquid-only diet when he discovered that he could no longer get onto his horse. He stayed in bed for several weeks, only allowing booze to pass his lips. The diet had mixed results. William once again mounted his horse – but consequently died soon afterwards in a riding accident and was still too obese to fit into his coffin at his funeral.

But it was at the beginning of the twentieth century that dieting really took off. In the vanguard was Horace Fletcher, the Chew-Chew Man, who declared – with admirable disregard for potential innuendo – that 'nature will castigate those who don't masticate'. He urged that all food should be chewed until it turned liquid and that food that would not become liquid should be removed from the mouth. This theory caused a few problems since it eliminated fibre from the diet of his followers and many of them began to suffer from constipation.

In the 1920s, Sylvia Ullbeck – a columnist on the popular gossip magazine *Photoplay* – advised a strict regime of calorie counting coupled with massages so forceful that 'fat comes through the pores like mashed potatoes through a colander'. Nice. But not as nice as the other favourite 1920s dieting favourite – encouraging a tape worm to grow in your own gut.

And so it went on. In the 1970s, poor Elvis tried the Sleeping Beauty Diet, getting doctors to put him to sleep for a few days in the hope that he would wake up thinner. Then he died fat and alone, eating a burger on the toilet. In the 1980s, slimmers put thinness before flatulence by restricting themselves to an intake of nothing more than cabbage soup. Current fads include the baby food diet, which is as self-explanatory as it is ridiculous (newborns and adults have very different dietary needs) and breatharianism.

Followers of this latter regime advocate living on light alone, saying that unpolluted air contains all the nutrients necessary to sustain life and that not eating food will actually increase a person's longevity. Of course, they're wrong and several followers have died in recent years while journalists have caught two of the regime's leading advocates buying chicken sandwiches and ordering meals on planes.

42

Get a Tattoo

....

The American comedian Richard Jeni said he always looked for a woman who had a tattoo: 'I see a woman with a tattoo,' he explained, 'and I'm thinking, OK, here's a gal who's capable of making a decision she'll regret in the future.'

The idea behind the joke actually has a sound statistical basis. Recent surveys by the American Society of Dermatological Surgery discovered that more than 50% of Americans with tattoos want theirs removed. The reasons vary from the horrifying realisation that Mötley Crüe aren't actually cool, to the hard lesson learned after that bastard P-A-T-R-I-C-K dumped me and I no longer H-E-A-R-T him. The common thread is the fact that the inks nearly always become marks of regret. Even those that weather the vagaries of love and fashion are no match for the cruelties of time. The designs we gouge into our pert skin when we're young come to symbolise the sad decay of age. Words blur, fade and lose all meaning. Pictures of faces grow wrinkled and haggard. Pretty little butterflies stretch into condors.

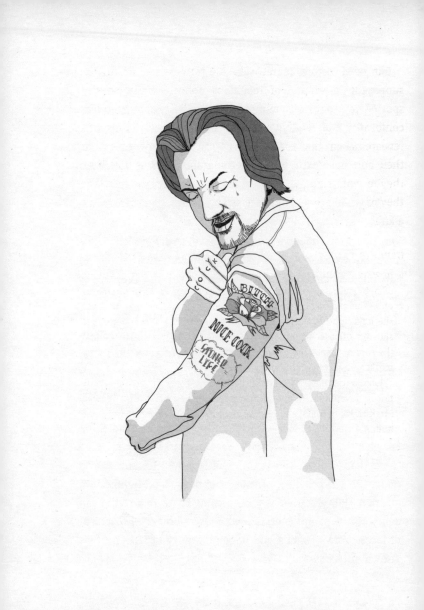

But even before regret sets in, tattoos are ridiculous: supposedly a symbol of rebellious nonconformity, they're sported nowadays with monotonous regularity and sheep-like conformity. Still, while it's easy to scoff at tattoo victims' oft-repeated claim that the formless Celtic swirl emerging from their butt hole 'expresses something about my personality', they're quite right. It does express something: the fact that they're willing to let complete strangers draw on them. With a knife.

USELESS TRIVIA

▶ In 2004, 19-year-old Joanne Raine paid £80 to have Roo, the name of her boyfriend, tattooed across her stomach in Chinese characters. The experience was something of a disaster. Firstly, because she later split up with her boyfriend. Secondly, because when she showed off the artwork in a Chinese restaurant a man behind the counter explained to her that she actually had the word 'supermarket' engraved on her body.

Joanne told the press: 'I did it because I wanted to show Roo how much I loved him... I did not think about whether it meant forever. I'm just going to have to keep it as I can't afford to get another one done.'

43

Join a Flash Mob

....

A flash mob is a large group of people who gather in a public place, perform a supposedly bizarre and surprising stunt and then quickly disperse. It's like happy slapping, without the physical violence but with the distinct lack of laughs for all involved.

The phenomenon took off during the summer of 2003 and unfortunately hasn't disappeared since. According to legend, the first incident occurred when a flash mob converged on the rug department of Macy's in New York City, gathered around a bit of carpet they called the 'love rug', told staff that they lived in a carpet warehouse commune and then disappeared again.

Other 'kkrrazzy' actions from a similar school of 'you can't stop me, I'm mad me' comedy have included a mass waving bananas, a collective shouting 'ahoy' at passing strangers and a 4,000 person strong music-free disco dancing session held on the passenger concourse of Victoria Station.

Flash mobs arrange to meet up using email and frequently film their activities, posting them up on the internet afterwards so we can all not laugh at them there as well.

Part of the joke seems to rely on the fact that members of the public who are unaware of the flash mobs' oh-so-mad plans will be completely bemused when the people around them start acting strangely. The trouble is that the concept has been so widely broadcast in recent years that no one will be surprised at all. Presumably the flash mobbers are expecting people to think: 'That's really weird! Oh! Hold my aching sides!' But naturally the most likely response is the recognition that: 'It's those flash mob knob-heads again,' and the heartfelt wish that they will hurry up and get out of the way.

A day spent taking part in a flash mob is a day spent interacting with a bunch of people who think that holding public pillow fights and walking around like zombies are art statements, followed by a lifetime of your idiocy preserved for all to see on YouTube.

USELESS TRIVIA

► Bill Wasik, the man credited with inventing flash mobs and that first stunt in Macy's, claims he came up with the idea to poke fun at 'hipsters' and their purposeless race to the next big trend. He says that he actually wanted to highlight the idiocy of the modern culture of conformity and described the trendsetting events he held around New York as 'completely absurd'. His point has been well made.

44

Play Second Life

If anything is likely to date this book horribly in a few years' time, it's this reference to a computer game that millions are playing now, but has every chance of being forgotten soon.

Second Life, for the benefit of those fortunate future generations who haven't had to read about it every day for the past two years in the fad-happy UK press, is an internet-based programme that allows users to create an 'avatar' version of themselves which they can then direct around a virtual world. In this brightly coloured electronic utopia they can buy property, watch adverts and spend money just like in real life, or, to use the slang of dedicated users, IRL. It's capitalism without the inconvenience of flesh, blood and smells.

There are certainly interesting philosophical questions raised by the fact that people will pay membership fees to have a digital second life when life in the real world is free and isn't infected by server lag, but it's surely a matter of time before the appeal of this shadow world fades. A world where every other person is either representing an evil multinational marketing department or is covered in digital fur or leather and insists on engaging you in mind-numbing semi-erotic conversation. A conversation that you're all too aware they are typing with one hand IRL, since they are using the other to furiously masturbate, tears of loneliness and self-hatred pouring down their pale, fleshy face all the while.

45

Shave All Your Hair Off

Going bald is presented to us in self-help books as a liberation. It's especially tempting to shave all your hair off if you're a man with long hair; not least because of the surprise effect it will have on your friends when the greasy mop disappears and your head suddenly looks like the top of a safety match. But the novelty is always short-lived. You will quickly realise your mistake, depending on how cold it is without hair or how easily the top of your delicate bonce burns in the sun. Either way, you will have to buy a hat and so defeat most of the object of losing your locks in the first place. The next three months will then be spent explaining to strangers that no, you aren't a fascist, and imagining that genuinely bald men are staring at you in jealous perplexity. Then, when your hair finally starts to grow back, you will look like a Lego man.

46

Visit the Whispering Gallery at St Paul's

....

There's no point denying that St Paul's cathedral itself, Sir Christopher Wren's greatest seventeenth-century masterpiece, is worth visiting. Its iconic dome and porticoed surrounds remain among wonders of the world and icons of London; it evokes the blitz spirit and every other deserved cliché relating to British architectural glory.

There is a need to point out, however, that no one should spoil their visit to the great church by bothering to obey all those guidebooks that tell you to visit the Whispering Gallery. Located just under the dome, at the top of 259 tiresome, claustrophobic steps, the gallery is said to be of interest because a word whispered into the wall at one side of its round balcony is supposed to be clearly audible on the other side. But it never is. All you are likely to hear is the furiously whispering child standing right next to you. That or the repeated complaints that 'I can't hear you!' made by all the other exhausted tourists who have schlepped up there and are now sharing the space with you, and have shortly before left their own biological imprint (in the form of mucus and disease) on the very piece of wall you are expected to press your lips against.

Admittedly, you get quite a nice view of the bottom of the cathedral and it's impressive enough for seventeenth-century technology – but now that we can get people on the phone half-way round the world, its value is questionable to say the least.

47

Get to Know
Your Neighbours

It's easy to lament the loss of community spirit in modern life and to fall into misty-eyed nostalgia for the days when everyone knew the names of everyone else on their own street.

The trouble is, as with most things for which we have nostalgia, the whole thing is an illusion. That halcyon good-neighbourly era never existed. The sepia-tinged, Hovis-advert-style terraced streets where everyone is chatting happily over the back fence are a myth. The reality was cruel gossip, curtain twitching, terrifying pressure towards social conformity and the daily necessity to engage in stultifying conversations about the weather with the nosy old lady at number 14. Those days were boring and everybody hated them. Why else do you think everyone was so ecstatic about the invention of the radio?

Getting to know your neighbours today is equally fraught with danger and potential tedium. What happens if they're violent psychos? What happens if they're religious? There will be no avoiding them in future. They're right beside you, seven days a week and they know exactly where you live.

USELESS TRIVIA

▶ The UK Home Office has estimated it spends £3.4 billion every year responding to reports of neighbourly antisocial behaviour.

48

Go to Koh Samui

....

This once idyllic island off the coast of Thailand provides a stark example of the dangers of following guidebooks and must-see recommendations.

Up until the middle of the twentieth century, this former paradise was self-sufficient and happily accommodated just 40,000 people. There wasn't even a road until the 1970s; around the same time that a few adventurous backpackers discovered the island's peaceful charms and began reporting back about the delights of long, empty white beaches, peaceful meals made from fish they'd caught themselves in its clean waters and serene coconut-tree-shaded quiet. Soon it was making the 'do before you die' lists. Less than 20 years later, it was a paradise lost.

Today, there is an international airport on Koh Samui and more than a million people visit every year. The coconut plantations have been infected with weevils, local marine life has been decimated and fish have to be imported. Tourists eat their meals in McDonald's and the streets are clogged with tattoo parlours, the kind of shops that sell T-shirts bearing the legend 'Life's a beach', and Irish pubs. Knife fights have broken out in the main Buddhist temple, and according to a 2006 article in the *Guardian*, there are three murders, three rapes and at least eight violent assaults there every year (all on a place the size of the Isle of Wight). Oh and there's no sewage system.

49

Get a Pet Cat

If you choose to spend your time with an animal that expresses its personality by torturing and slowly killing cute little baby voles and precious wild birds, that's entirely up to you. Many people even claim that stroking a cat is good for the blood pressure and that having these psychopathic companions is wonderful for your own psychic well-being.

But here's the thing about cats: they never share your pleasure. They only extract pleasure from you. They don't give a stuff about your own feelings. The only reason a cat would give your death a second thought would be because it's considering whether to chow down on your corpse.

USELESS TRIVIA

▶ There are around 10 million cats in the UK. One in four of them is obese. In spite of this fact, the Mammal Society estimates that our feline friends still manage to kill 300 million other small animals every year. Roy Hattersley, the Labour MP, denounced cats as evil because of the devastating effect they have on Britain's wild birds. Then his dog Buster was caught killing a goose in a royal park.

50

Touch a Tiger

If you're daft enough to want to touch a tiger, you probably deserve everything that's coming to you in terms of teeth, sharp claws and ravening maws.

However, let me appeal at least to your respect for the poor animal's dignity. Imagine you were one of the last 200 humans on the earth and thousands of representatives of the species that has all but wiped you out insisted on stroking *your* bottom. And all because some lifestlye guru has told them it will be 'spiritually enriching'. Believe me, the best thing most of us can do for tigers is leave the poor sods alone.

USELESS TRIVIA

▶ The collective noun for tigers is 'an ambush'. A fact that has nothing to do with anything, but remains kind of cool.

51

Touch a Member of the Royal Family

···

Nowadays, no one believes that touching one of the Royal Family can cure the 'King's evil', and their services would only rarely be required anyway, because the disfiguring and potentially fatal disease of scrofula has all but disappeared since the beginning of the twentieth century. Nonetheless, the Royal Family remains with us and some set considerable store by being in their presence. But even for those eager to get up close and personal with the Windsors, attempting to make physical contact with them is not advised. It's apparently considered bad etiquette to extend a hand to 'Ma'am' before she deigns to reach her own out to you – and thanks to the large number of armed security officers who accompany her everywhere she goes, potentially even more dangerous than touching a tiger.

► Scrofula is the name given to a variety of skin diseases affecting the lymph nodes in the neck so that they swell up, start looking horrible and then kill you. In the Middle Ages, kings were thought to have the power to cure it, handed down to them in a bloodline from Edward the Confessor who in turn picked up the skill from Saint Remigius. They didn't.

52

Learn to Play the Ukulele

In an outbreak of whackiness not seen since Timmy Mallet dominated the airwaves, ukulele playing has recently become inexplicably popular in the UK. Despicable lifestyle journalists have made it their mission to foist these 'bonsai guitars' onto the nation, while every other gig seems to feature an 'ironic' ukulele-based cover version of 'Smells Like Teen Spirit' or 'Purple Haze'.

The advocates of this dangerous build-up proclaim that the instrument is delightfully simple to play and that you very quickly begin to feel 'at one' with it.

What they neglect to mention is that it sounds absolutely dreadful.

Even played well, the instrument infests every tune it touches with a laughless comedy twang – an irritation factor that humour-desert George 'oooh mother' Formby well understood when he tortured the world with an arsenal of the things back in the 1930s. It wasn't funny then and it certainly isn't funny now. It's time for 'uklear disarmament'.

53

Go to See the *Mona Lisa*

....

There's definitely something about the *Mona Lisa*'s enigmatic smile. There isn't much likelihood of its position as one of the world's most revered paintings being threatened soon either. The 6 million people who visit it every year can't all be entirely wrong, after all. But what they can all be is damn annoying. Especially when they're standing in front of you, holding up their camera at just the right angle to prevent you seeing anything other than a minuscule digital recreation of the precious picture.

Queuing to see Leonardo Da Vinci's most famous creation in the Louvre is no more uplifting than waiting to check in for an aeroplane – and generally takes far longer. The reward at the end of all that waiting, pushing and jostling to get a good viewing position is tiny. Literally. The painting is so small it's extremely hard to make out any detail at the distance you have to remain from it for security reasons. It also comes in unexpectedly drab shades of yellow and brown (most reproductions are spruced up) thanks to the cruel effects of time on its protective varnish. It's such a disappointing sight that, after queuing for hours, the vast majority of the 70 tourists a minute who file in to do obeisance before the *Mona Lisa* only remain in front of her for a maximum of 15 seconds.

If the mysterious woman in the picture knew her fate, she wouldn't just be smiling, she'd be laughing.

54

Shop on Carnaby Street

One of the surest ways you can tell that the writers of your guidebook haven't actually been to London, and are making it up as they go along, is if they recommend a visit to Carnaby Street.

Once reputed to be the haunt of Paul McCartney, Mick Jagger, Jimi Hendrix and just about everyone who was anyone in the late 1960s, this famous street is often portrayed as the counterculture in concrete form, a kind of Diagon Alley of hippy clothes, a place of magical possibility for anyone keen to get into the sway of swinging London.

Now, like Sir Thumbs Aloft and most of his fashionable friends, it's seen better days. The thriving centre of alternative culture has been covered over with flagship stores for American labels and is filled only with tourists who are bewildered by the distinct lack of cool stuff and who, by their very presence, diminish yet further from any hip cachet that the place might have had. It's worth visiting only if you want a hard, cold lesson in the sad reality of global capitalism and how The Man will always defeat and commodify the flower children.

▶ The fact that guidebook writers – even the most reputable – don't always visit the locations they are writing about was confirmed by former Lonely Planet contributor Thomas Kohnstamm who confessed in his book *Do Travel Writers Go To Hell* that he helped to produce one of the Lonely Planet guides to Columbia while 'in San Francisco', and took other information about locations from the internet. When he did actually visit places he had some quite exciting experiences, however. He boasts elsewhere in his book that in one restaurant he was reviewing, he had sex with a waitress after all the other customers had left. He then went on in his guide to say that the same restaurant 'is a pleasant surprise... and the table service is friendly.'

55

Walk from Land's End to John o'Groats

There are all sorts of reasons why walking 1,000 hilly miles in the British weather is inadvisable, but the most important is the necessity of walking through the West Midlands and Staffordshire. Stopping there for anything other than petrol borders on insanity. It's bad enough crawling through it on the M6, let alone trudging every rain-sodden inch and potentially letting yourself in for having to spend a night in Tamworth.

USELESS TRIVIA

▸ As every pub quiz stalwart will be able to tell you, John o'Groats is not actually the northernmost point of mainland Scotland. That honour lies with Dunnet Head, a few miles to the west. Meanwhile, the point furthest from Land's End (which is at least the most westerly point on the British mainland) is Duncansby Head, a couple of miles further along the coast from John o'Groats. The habit of walking to John o'Groats instead of either of these two other points appears to be a continuation of a mistake made by the first person to complete the route in 1879, Robert Carlyle, a Cornishman who – interestingly enough – pushed a wheelbarrow the entire way.

56

Go to a
Nudist Beach

....

We're told it's liberating, but really going naked in public just gives us one more thing to worry about; especially on the beach where the issues of sand in your sandwiches and salt in your hair will come as light relief.

If it's a nice day, you'll burn your bits. If it's not, your bits will beat an undignified retreat.

On top of all that, you'll be made to feel physically inferior by all the beautiful creatures showing off their perfect bodies around you. Conversely, if you are lucky enough to be good-looking*, you'll just spend the whole day being ogled at by physically inferior people.

And that's before we've even thought about the problems surrounding large ageing fellows called Gunther...

---

* *You git.*

57

Listen to Oasis's *Definitely Maybe*

....

If this album is, as we're so frequently informed by the music press, the one that defined the 1990s, then the 1990s was a pint of wife-beater lager.

58

Join the Mile High Club

Joining the mile high club has become such a cliché that it now seems as risqué as Marks & Spencer. But it's nothing like as convenient. The main differences between having sex flying in a plane and sex on the ground are that in a plane you have to do it in a toilet that is barely big enough to stand up in and there's a far higher probability of rubbing your squashy parts against surfaces where someone else has recently vomited. Or worse.

It's also worth noting that in most planes nowadays an alarm sounds if anyone stays locked in the loo for more than 15 minutes and the cabin crew come along and open them up. This is potentially even more embarrassing than staying in for less than the allotted time.

USELESS TRIVIA

► The first people said to have joined the mile high club were Lawrence Sperry and Mrs Waldo Polk in 1916. Their amorous escapades severely disrupted the flight of a Curtiss flying boat, perhaps not surprisingly considering Lawrence Sperry was also the plane's pilot and was supposed to be taking it over New York at the time. After the plane inevitably crashed, duck hunters discovered the couple butt naked but still alive in South Bay, New York. The New York tabloid *Mirror & Evening Graphic*, reported the incident with the headline: 'AERIAL PETTING – ENDS IN WETTING'. Probably not coincidentally, Lawrence Sperry is also credited with the invention of the first aeroplane autopilot.*

---

* *Honestly! True fact!*

59

Suck Up to God

....

Even if you buy into Pascal's wager and agree that the philoso-
pher was right when he said that belief in God is a gamble
worth taking, why assume that getting on your knees and
praying to him is the best way to win his favours? No one else
likes a kiss-ass, so why should He?

60

Conquer Your Worst Fear

....

The too-often repeated advice that you should confront your worst fear head-on is sensible only if you are afraid of cute little ponies, making oodles and oodles of lovely money or similarly harmless or potentially beneficial aspects of life.

If, in contrast, your worst fear is being trapped inside an elevator with Jeremy Clarkson while the building around you burns and chlorine gas seeps through the doors, attempting to get up close and personal with it will bring only pain. The same is true if you are afraid of being in a plane crash, drowning, running into a hail of machine-gun fire or having your naughty bits eaten by rats.

Most of our fears are quite sensible and potentially life-saving. Don't scorn them. Embrace them. They might just save your life.

61

Ensure Your Place in History

....

Who are the most famous people ever? Hitler, Stalin, Ghengis Khan, William the Conqueror, Attila the Hun, Henry VIII, Peter the Great, Nero, Caligula, Madonna. What do they have in common? They are all massively evil cunts.

The only way to ensure immortality is by being far badder than everyone else... Or get shot, or otherwise martyred like the second rung of famous historical figures: John Lennon, Gandhi and John F Kennedy.

62

Visit Tuvalu

....

This clutch of South Pacific islands is predicted to be among the early victims of global warming. As the sea level rises, the low-lying land (none of it more than five metres above sea level) will be swamped and we can all say goodbye to this South Sea paradise of coconut groves, blue lagoons, internet entrepreneurs (Tuvalu has the nifty domain name '.tv') and, thanks to quirks of the international telephone leasing system and its expensively exotic location, naughty phone lines.

Scientists say it could all disappear as soon as 2050. So, say the list-makers, if you visit soon you'll be able to tell your descendants that you've been somewhere they will never be able to go. You've walked on the (admittedly less glamorous) modern-day equivalent of Atlantis. Which sounds pretty cool, until the moment those same descendants ask you why. Or what on earth you did when you got there.

The trouble with Tuvalu is not only that it's almost as boring as Easter Island (see p.47), there's also the hugely embarrassing conversations you might have to engage in with the remaining locals in the island's one bar. What, after all, can you say to someone whose imminent misery you've come to gawp at? Do you apologise for the fact that you've just added to the problem by flying all the way out there? Buying him a beer and inviting him to drown his sorrows probably won't go down too well either...

63

Have a New Species
Named After You

....

This is yet another superficially appealing idea rendered ridiculous as soon as you actually think about it. Obeying the list makers and trying to achieve this goal is a fools' errand rivalled only by attempting to apply your name to a star (see p.22).

This time, the main problem is that all the good animals have already been taken. While it would be pretty cool to have creatures as splendid as elephants walking around bearing your name, the only things scientists are likely to find in the near future are malformed bottom-dwellers deep in the salty bowels of the earth or new mutant forms of bacteria.

There are also difficult practical issues. In order to have something named after you, you either have to become or befriend one of the people who do the world's species categorisation – taxonomists. Sadly, these are generally serious professionals who consider it bad form to give creatures dappy names on a vainglorious whim. That's why there aren't hundreds of species of John Smith and Joe Bloggs out there and most animals have vaguely meaningful monikers. Even supposing you go to all the trouble of exploring the furthest reaches of the rainforests and bringing back a never-before-seen insect, it's unlikely to be given your name.

Meanwhile, the idea is not only almost impossible, but it's also impossibly foolish. If for the sake of argument we accept that all the above mentioned practical problems could be overcome and you do manage to put your name to a previously unknown form of life, who's to say it won't go on to bring shame on you? You won't feel so proud if that rare bacterium is brought out of the jungle depths and goes on to wipe out all the pretty little bunny rabbits in the world, will you? Nor if, as is more likely, it turns out to be utterly boring and pointless.

64

Read Wordsworth

....

Let's not beat about the bush. 'Daffodils' is a crap poem. For a
start, clouds are rarely lonely, especially in Cumbria. Secondly,
who cares if Wordsworth saw some flowers? Thirdly, and for
all sorts of reasons, the following is surely one of the most
painful rhymes in the English language:

> A poet could not but be gay,
> In such a jocund company.

65

Go Zorbing

....

Zorbing entered the *Concise Oxford English Dictionary* in 2001 where it was defined as: 'A sport in which a participant is secured inside an inner capsule in a large transparent ball which is then rolled along the ground or down hills.'

The same dictionary defines sport as: 'an activity involving physical exertion and skill in which an individual or team competes against another or others.' Either we are to presume that there's some skill in being pushed down a hill while you're strapped inside a big football, or dictionary makers can sometimes be as sloppy as compilers of lists.

Whatever.

As the websites offering to let you try this stomach-churning Antipodean pastime in the UK say, the idea of being pushed down a hill inside a gigantic inflatable sphere may seem crazy to some – but that's because it is. Especially given the fact that one of the most popular variants on the 'sport' is to descend the hill in a sphere half-filled with water. For those keen to learn what it's like inside a washing machine, that may be considered a useful life experience. For others, it's a

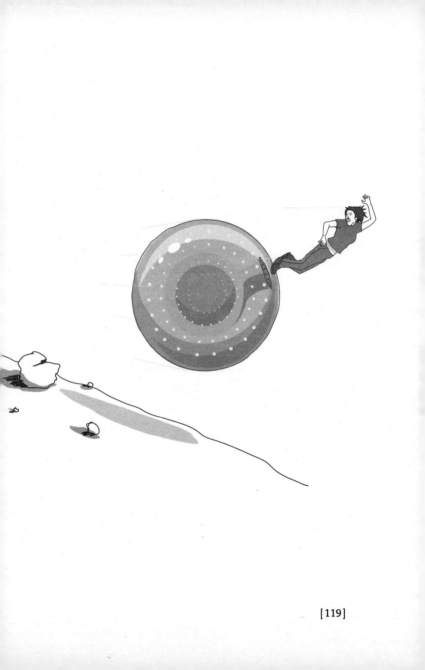

damning indictment of their time on earth. How wasted has their life been that they consider trundling down a muddy slope strapped inside a giant, wet football an improvement?

66

Run Barefoot in Central Park

....

Jane Fonda may have persuaded Robert Redford to throw off his shoes in the 1960s romantic comedy *Barefoot in the Park*, but following suit will not – as life gurus suggest – display your happiness and liberation. All it actually displays is your willingness to stand on broken glass and have your tootsies stabbed by needles. There's a reason modern urban man wears shoes: to keep dog shit off his feet.

67

Look at Things Differently

....

Don't just think outside the box. Question why it has to be a box at all! Changing your view of the world is as simple as putting on bright pink socks! Take a coffee cup. Turn it upside down. Imagine how its function might be impaired by being upside down. But what can it do that it couldn't do before? Why not draw the cup? But with your left hand! (Or your right if you're left-handed! Don't cheat now!!) So you get that gritty naivety. Break the cup! Hide it! (Like a dog with a bone.) Imagine it's not a cup. It's a door! Why call it a door? Isn't it rather a portal? Or is it in fact a jar? What's on the other side of the door? Another door? Or the rest of the world? Imagine yourself being the door. Consider the bigger picture. If you have a problem, why not stand on a ladder and look down at it from there. Or look at it from the other side of the door! Imagine yourself from very far away looking at things that are now very up close and personal. Get some emotional distance. Don't cry at death. Laugh! Every laugh makes you feel better and makes angels sing. Stand the world on its head. No! Wait! Stand on your own head! Which is the wrong way round now?

You or the world? Why do you even look to get your point of view? Why not use your other senses? Why not try to listen to what's on the other side of the doors (portals) of perception? Or smell it? What's there? Your cup which you hid! Pick up the (broken) cup again. Now throw it out the window and stop acting like a knob.

68

Take a Shower in a Waterfall

It's not pleasant to shower in a waterfall. Generally, they are bloody cold and flow so fast that it hurts. Life is not a shampoo advert. And if you do manage to use shampoo in a waterfall, you'll help pollute its plunge pool and the rest of the river, thereby destroying the very pristine beauty you're supposed to be enjoying. As will your bloodied corpse when 2,000 gallons of high-pressure water blasts you off your feet and down to a wet, and probably deserved, death.

USELESS TRIVIA

▶ There are no reliable death by waterfall statistics out there, although a recent study has suggested that they are far more of a threat to mankind than has previously been assumed. *Death in Yosemite*, Michael P Ghiglieri and Charles R 'Butch' Farabee Jr's gripping account of all the people that have snuffed it in the famous US national park, contains accounts of various waterfalls around the Yosemite Valley slaying an astonishing 42 people between 1913 and 2006. That's more than Charles Manson and Dr Crippen combined.

69

Visit Florence

Admittedly this ornate Italian city worked hard to earn its reputation as the cradle and heart of the Renaissance, but that was also the time Florence was last interesting. Since Michelangelo died in 1564 the place has been dull enough to bore everyone else into the afterlife too.

The brightly decorated shell of the city remains, but any authentic talent has long since fled to be replaced by a certain type of too-wealthy American on sabbatical from squashing heads on the college football field or impatient to 'do the Uffizi' while storming round 'Yurp' in a frenzy of shopping, 'culture' and complaints about the prices of hotel rooms. It is, consequently, also just about the only place in Italy where you can buy bad coffee.

USELESS TRIVIA

▶ Stendhal Syndrome is the name given to a psychosomatic illness that affects visitors to Florence. It is characterised by rapid heartbeats, confusion, dizziness and (in extreme cases) hallucinations. These symptoms are generally said to be caused by an intoxicating overexposure to fine art, but a far more likely explanation is that victims are simply overcome by overexposure to the city's furnace-like heat, crowds of braying tourists and overpriced pizzas.

70

Be Happy

....

The world's a mess. The ocean levels are rising. Blood is flowing faster than oil in the Middle East. A shady conspiracy of multinational environmental criminals has wrested control of the world's wealth from our elected representatives. Our elected representatives, meanwhile, are all idiots and bastards. There still isn't a cure for heart failure and most of the food you enjoy eating is poisonous. The only things that are guaranteed in life are death, taxes and 99% of everything shown on TV being crap.

In short, happiness is an entirely unrealistic reaction to the human condition. An absurdly optimistic denial of basic facts. So don't let anyone try to suggest you're doing something wrong or you're somehow a failure if you remain a bit glum. Melancholy is a sign of considerable self-awareness. What's more, those who have embraced it have produced some of our finest art.

Had Beethoven started taking Prozac, we might never have heard the 'Eroica' symphony. Van Gogh might have kept both his ears if he'd gone on a self-help binge and found his 'inner smile', but we'd never have heard of him, let alone had pictures to brighten our own lives. John Keats, John Lennon*, Franz Kafka, Ian Curtis, Kurt Cobain: all miserable sods – and all the better for it. The sad people make the world a happier place. It's the happy, simple ones like George Bush, Uncle Joe Stalin and Ronald McDonald who spread the hurt.

---

* John Lennon was actually briefly happy, when he recorded the album Double Fantasy. Anyone who has heard the song 'Dear Yoko' will understand that that was not necessarily a good thing.

71

Panic *

....

The world may be a mess, but that's no reason to make it worse for yourself by seeing terrorists on every tube train and murder in every mosque. Contrary to what we're told about national security situations, outside threats and the need to stockpile tins and head for the hills, the statistical chances of living to old age in the twenty-first century are greater than ever before (for most of us, at least).

In a deliciously cruel twist of fate there's even considerable statistical evidence that those who worry most die youngest. Those who stress about burglars, muggers, caffeine levels, alcohol and the dangers of too much fun, and who therefore spend their time installing alarms, avoiding walks in the park and drinking herbal tea, generally suffer from cancer and stress-related heart disease far earlier than those who don't give a crap. Life is cruel, but there's little you can do about it, so you might as well fill it with pleasure instead of worry.

---

* See Appendix 1.

▸ Interestingly, in World War II, when the shit really *was* hitting the fan, the media and government tried to encourage the exact opposite reaction to the one they do now. The UK government even ran a poster campaign featuring the splendid words: 'Keep Calm and Carry On'. They presumably didn't feel the need to keep on reminding us about the terror threat when bombs were genuinely falling every day.

72

Get Rich

The old cliché that money doesn't buy happiness might not be entirely true. As Spike Milligan pointed out, it does at least bring you a more pleasant form of misery. What's more, it's probably far better to be rich than it is to follow that other stock piece of self-help advice and dispose of all your material possessions. It is at least easier to contemplate being cheerful than it is living in your own shit and begging for food.

All the same, there is considerable statistical evidence to suggest that material wealth isn't all it's cracked up to be. There's even a name for a strand of thought which suggests that money does nothing to make you feel better once you have enough to satisfy your basic needs: 'The Easterlin Paradox'.

Easterlin was an economist who discovered that even though wealth grew dramatically in Japan during the post-war economic boom between 1950 and 1970, life satisfaction fell. The Japanese might have been able to buy more, but they were also more miserable.

Several later theories have backed this up – and simulta-neously belied that frequent addition to the aforementioned cliché that those who think money doesn't buy happiness just don't know where to shop.

The old-fashioned economic theory of well-being used to be that those who had more wealth-related options were likely to feel better generally. That's to say that those who don't have any financial concern about what they pick off a menu are likely to be more cheery than those who have to limit themselves to a starter and a glass of water – or aren't allowed in the restaurant at all.

But repeated studies have shown that having too much actual choice leaves people on edge and with a lingering worry, once they have made their selection, that they could have gone for something better. Meanwhile, wants for luxury items very quickly become needs. Rich people, apparently, actually think they can't get by without that ridiculous four-wheel drive, sending their hateful children to schools that teach them how to talk like a 1930s BBC radio announcer and wearing silly gold lamé clothes at Ascot.

Tied in with all that is the fact that rich people are far more likely to be overworked and overtired than those on lower incomes. Statistics from the US Bureau of Labor [sic] prove that those who earn more have to do more chores and have less fun. American men who make over $100,000 a year spend 19.9% of their time kicking back and relaxing, watching TV or socialising. Those on less than $20,000 gave over a much more pleasant 34.7% of their time to passive leisure, and far less to working, commuting, or carrying out chores like shopping. They were also found to be under far less stress and tension.

All of which begs the question of what's the point having all that lolly if you aren't going to be able to enjoy it; you still die just the same and everyone you meet starts to assume that you're either a posh tosser or a corporate thief.

So much for the theories, however. You could easily be forgiven if you've read this much of the entry and still aren't convinced.* There aren't many of us who would turn down the chance of a cool million or so, after all. And there aren't many of us who won't imagine that it might improve our lives. But just consider this: the richest woman in England is the Queen. And she hasn't smiled since 1968.

---

* *You can also be forgiven if you suspect the author of even more rank hypocrisy than normal. He is forced to admit – dear reader – that making him (stinking) rich comes a lot higher on his list of best-case scenario outcomes for this book than improving your life. Even making you laugh he considers as merely a happy side effect to an imagined new-found ability to buy a gleaming new Moulton bicycle. He would probably also give higher priority to surprising his old school friends with his new-found toilet-book fame, walking into Waterstone's and not having the embarrassment of having to get someone to look up his name on the stock computer before he can locate the one copy of Sod That! in the store, and annoying Jeremy Clarkson. He apologises, bows and hopes you are enjoying yourself nevertheless.*

73

Take Part in a Moonlit Drum Circle

....

Blithely ignoring the fact that there's little evidence that our ancestors actually ever elected to indulge in night-time arrhythmic arms-aloft dancing and bongo whacking, exponents of moonlit drum circles insist they are a good way to reconnect with the ancients. Drumming, we are told, is a powerful spiritual tool. It has been used 'since the beginning of time' to energise, empower, create wholeness and heighten creativity. It helps us to reconnect with our origins! It facilitates the forging of spiritual bridges with the original walkers of the planet, the indigenous people of the earth!

But if you really want to get back to your prehistoric roots, the best thing to do is throw out your shoes, take up residence in a cave, start living off roots and watch your family get eaten by bears. At least that way you'll avoid the necessity of talking to someone called Pragit about his chakra.

74

Go to a Gig

You spend hours queuing at the bar, get to the front and buy flat lager in a plastic glass for £4.50. Out on the dark, smelly dancefloor you realise that the music is nothing like as good as the finely honed studio versions and its volume is about to make your ears bleed. You also realise that you're standing next to a person who thinks that urinal is a posh word for Y-fronts and insists on singing along with every song, thus marring what little enjoyment you have been gaining from the music that you can hear above the squeal of feedback.

Then, someone will kick you in the face while attempting to crowd-surf. That isn't much fun either.

75

Eat Sturgeon Caviar

....

When people start telling you that the metallic taste of even a silver spoon will destroy a food's taste, it's a sure sign that you're entering a zone of high-grade bullshit. How little flavour do these oily fish periods have if you can't taste them over a piece of cutlery? Have you ever detected the metallic tang of a spoon on any other occasion? Meanwhile, even if one accepts the absurd possibility that the metal taste does make a difference, wouldn't a simple plastic implement be a far better alternative than the usually offered mother-of-pearl obscenity? Than a spoon that costs more than most families' monthly food budget? Conversely, if the flavour were so precious and delicate why does everyone wash it down with the strong, lingering taste of champagne?

All that the spoon and bubbly snobbery really add is another layer of flummery to an already ridiculous food ceremony. Eating caviar is not a gourmet experience; it's just an ostentatious display of how much money you are prepared to convert into shit. Which is fine if you are an over-rich, over-compensating tosser, but rather undignified if you are not.

▶ Sturgeon, the gentle prehistoric fish from which the caviar eggs are ripped, are on the verge of extinction thanks to chronic overfishing, poaching and pollution.

76

Learn
Survival Skills

....

It is a truth universally acknowledged that survival skills are useful in the modern world. But although we are so often and so piously informed that wilderness skills are not just helpful, but crucial to our well-being, we're never really told why. In what kind of situation, say, is the preferred bushcraft fire-lighting method of rubbing a piece of *Daldinia concentrica* fungus against dry grass for half an hour going to be more practical than using matches? In what kind of world is that fungus going to be easier to find than a cigarette lighter? And do you really want to take advice from someone who claims to be a wilderness sage but can't even remember to pack the Swan Vestas?

Discounting the idea that the best longevity insurance is to stay inside and not go anywhere dangerous in the first place, survival courses do at least offer to free us from the shackles of modern life – but again it's debatable how free you are when you have to spend the whole day foraging around to fulfil the basic needs of food and shelter. Needs that are generally laid on at home anyway, without the risk of waking up to discover that you've been sleeping on an ant's nest.

Pessimistic backwoodsmen could potentially argue that there is the whole economic collapse, global warming Armageddon scenario, but if the world does melt down to the extent that we're no longer able to pop down the shops for food, it's by no means certain that trapping and skinning a (presumably now highly toxic) rabbit is going to be top of anyone's priorities. Not compared to finding a tin-opener and a good stash of baked beans anyway – items that true survival experts are always going to prefer to Stone Age boat-making tools and beds made out of moss.

USELESS TRIVIA

► A 2007 *Esquire* survey discovered that television bushcraft expert Ray Mears is the third most admired man in the UK. The winner of the survey was Gordon Ramsay. Enough said.

77

Run With the Bulls in Pamplona

When the half-dozen bucking and furious mountains of beef are released into the crowded streets of Pamplona during the annual bull run, the average participant's adrenaline levels double and his or her heart rate triples, supplying a massive mind-zonking primeval high. Many claim that it is the closest you can get to our prehistoric roots and the exciting feeling of being pursued by a sabre-toothed tiger, happily ignoring the issue that Stone Age man almost certainly did everything he could to avoid such encounters and thus guaranteed our longevity as a species. If, like you, our hairy ancestors had the option of not putting themselves in grave danger, they'd almost certainly have used their Spanish holiday to go to the beach and drink Rioja.

The sad fact about the Pamplona festival is also that you aren't running *with* the bulls, you're running with hundreds of thousands of half-cut Ernest Hemingway imitators. The bulls themselves are running in spite of all the people blocking their way. They are frightened, disorientated and only moving so fast because they are in a panic about getting back to their herd.

► Many think that it is good luck to touch the bull during the run. But all too often they prove this theory wrong by getting a horn up their backside. Dozens are gored every year and since 1924, 15 people have been killed. No one's been counting how many bulls have copped it.

78

Go to Lourdes

....

If you enjoy witnessing the financial exploitation of the sick and desperate, Lourdes is the place for you. If you're lucky, you may also get to see one of those huge pile of crutches and walking aids left behind after God has cured the lame, and wonder: why are there never any prosthetic limbs in these piles? Does God hate amputees? Or is there something else going on? No matter. There's a whole Catholic Disneyland to take in yet!

If you are able to make your way through the thick crowds (not necessarily easy in a town of 15,000 inhabitants which is visited by more than 6 million people every year), you have an astonishing array of religiously themed gift stores to take in. There you can buy Virgin Mary key rings, Virgin Mary sweeties, Saint Bernadette cigarette lighters, plastic saintly grottoes and Jesus snow domes. Then, if all that wears you out, take in a nice cooling drink in the Immaculate Conception ice-cream parlour.

But don't stay out too late, though, because the religious tourists of Lourdes have been known to cause so much drunken violence in the streets that local *gendarmes* have proclaimed themselves unable to cope and called in the *Compagnies républicaines de sécurité*, the notorious French riot police who now carry out late night patrols around the town's hundreds of bars and clubs.

USELESS TRIVIA

▸ The otherwise unremarkable town of Lourdes, notable only for its situation on a convenient route node in the foothills of the Pyrenees, began its climb to fame on 11 February 1858, when 14-year-old Bernadette Soubirous claimed to have seen the first of 18 apparitions of the Virgin Mary in a cave usefully close to the town centre. She was only the latest in a long line of girls in the area to bring attention to herself by claiming to have a chat with the mythical mother of Jesus, but she was unique in the excitement her series of tête-à-têtes created, especially after the story got about that the Virgin Mary had caused a spring to appear in the cave – and that its waters had healing properties. No one else saw the vision – but the rest of the locals did at least have the foresight to realise that the story was a great way of making money. Young Bernadette had barely left the cave by the time her family was setting up the town's biggest and most expensive hotel and the true miracle – the one involving the huge numbers of highly profitable visitors – was taking shape. Sadly, the young girl herself didn't have much chance to enjoy the bounty. As her fame grew, she was ushered away to a monastery and died in agony aged just 35, a lasting testimony to the inefficacy of the waters that so many poor saps are conned into sampling every year.

79

Read the Bible as Literature

....

Contrary to popular belief, the Bible is not a good book. Even if one ignores its malign social influence, scientific absurdity, historical implausibility and the rather sordid origins of Christian orthodoxy, it's still a pretty bad piece of work. It is not, as is so often claimed, a collection of stories worth perusing as quality literature alone and there's little point in bothering trying to read it as such.

The high quality of the Bible as a work or literary art is up there with the fine needlework on the Emperor's New Clothes as something that nobody dares question. However, why not freely state the obvious, but hitherto rarely mentioned, truth? The majority of the 1,000-plus pages of the Bible do not comprise, as is so often suggested, a damn good read. They're crap. If the two Testaments tell the greatest story ever told, we are all monkeys (and not just the distant descendants of them).

OK, it's possible to concede that there are a few passages of extraordinary power and beauty in the Bible. The Song of Solomon, for instance, is as impressive as it is kinky. There's also no more striking an example of random and bizarre sadism in literature than God's decision to turn Lot's wife into a pillar of salt and then make the luckless widower have sex with his daughters in a cave. The Book of Revelation, meanwhile, is an hallucinogenic head-trip without parallel from start to finish: exhilarating, unsettling and gloriously mad.

However, these are rare flashes of light in 1,000-plus pages of opaque, dull, greyness. Could anyone really enjoy reading all those lists of endless genealogies that take up such huge portions of the Old and such hefty chunks of the New Testaments? Has anyone got the stamina to read the entire tedious work from cover to cover? To keep up with all those hundreds of characters that appear from nowhere and disappear without explanation, rhyme or reason (the greatest story thereby displaying ignorance of the most basic storytelling rules)?

Do all the cubits, marriages, lists of names, departures, camps in the plains of Moab across from Jericho and offerings of goats say more to you about the human condition than, say, *The Great Gatsby*? Would you even prefer to read all that bunk about demons in the New Testament, unleavened as it is by humour or the intriguing possibility of the lead character finally losing his virginity, to *Harry Potter*?

In short, does anyone sincerely believe that the vast majority of the Bible is anything other than crashingly dull? Discounting the pretty slim possibility that labouring through the Testaments may win you a pass card to Heaven, there is no reward to be gained from trudging through this messy ancient hodgepodge. You haven't failed if you haven't read it; you've just avoided a lot of boredom and a few weird moments of torture and incest.

80

Rebel

....

Teddy boys, hippies, punks, ravers. The only thing succeeding generations of youthful rebels really prove is how ineffectual the last must have been at making the world a better place. Extreme haircuts, sloppy dressing and I-won't-tidy-my-bedroom politics do not a revolution make. All that people become after years of fighting The Man is tired. Worn down by the drugs, deafened by the music, fatigued by long marches that go nowhere and change nothing, they end up being yet more reactionary than the people they originally hated.

The only Teddy Boy who's still earning a living is Cliff Richard. It's the peace and love hippy generation who gave us Margaret Thatcher, Tony Blair, George Bush and the never-ending war on terror. The repeated appearances of ex-punks have ensured Jools Holland's offensively bland boogie-woogie honky tonk is the only long-running music programme on British TV. Julie Burchill's found God and Johnny Rotten appears on early-evening ITV reality shows. A few former ravers and poll tax rioters still nostalgically spin the perhaps over-optimistic 1990s dance hit 'Hardcore Will Never Die' and dress up in boiler suits at the weekend, but most work in call centres.

Genuine change is generally brought about by people who keep a low profile in their youth, dress with military rigour, cultivate a liking for traditional music and appeal to the middle classes who then venerate them as national saviours. People like Hitler. They suck too.

81

Wear a Diamond

No matter how expensive your diamond is, it will always look cheap. Wearing a big rock is to discretion what herds of elephants are to meadows of delicate wild flowers. It's no less than a glitzy, public demonstration of your bank account details – or perhaps how much your partner is prepared to part with for sex. There is, admittedly, a certain appeal in a diamond's all-enduring, tool-grinding hardness, but as Henry Kissinger has pointed out, they remain nothing more than a chunk of coal that's made good under pressure.

82

Swim the English Channel

Swimming all the way across the English Channel is as close as you can get to the fun of drowning without actually dying. But that's not to say that crossing one of the world's busiest shipping lanes isn't without its perils. Aside from the fact that it is cold, subject to strong tidal changes every six hours and rank with pollution, the narrow stretch of water between Britain and France plays host to 600 commercial ship movements and more than 80 ferry crossings every day – all of which present unwelcome hazards to anyone silly enough to get in the water.

All the same, this feat of endurance is not at all interesting. And that's in spite of the many dubious novelties the Channel swim presents. True, there are few other opportunities or reasons in life to cover yourself with goose grease. It's also rare that you are fed your food from a pole on a moving boat. Few of us have many opportunities to detour around shoals of stinging, pollution-ridden jellyfish. And even fewer of us have had the experience of having our lives threatened by floating timbers or fridges.

No, much like Formula One racing, the cold swim between England and France manages to warp the laws of nature and be both dangerous and boring. The equivalent of swimming 700 lengths of an Olympic swimming pool, it generally takes more than ten hours to complete and is as dull as only 21 miles of ditchwater can be. It is, therefore, not surprising to learn that only 10% of swimmers complete the crossing. It is also not surprising to learn that this feat of endurance and bloody-minded refusal to admit the superiority of boats as a means of conveyance across water is frequently called 'the Everest of open water swimming' (see p.5).

83

Do It in the Road

....

'Why don't we do it in the road?' asked Paul McCartney on The Beatles' *White Album*. Self-help authors ever since have been agreeing that the suggestion might be worth taking up. But there are several painfully obvious answers to the question: whoever's underneath will pick up all kinds of nasty scratches and friction burns; you might get arrested; you might get squashed. Paul Cowley and Kim Fontana are the most recent couple to have proved this point when they started having sex on a road in Sheffield on 3 March 2002 and were run over by a bus and pressed like a pair of trousers.

84

Vote

....

No matter whom you vote for, the government always gets in. So sang the Bonzo Dog Band – and there's no disagreeing with them. Governments are universally awful and the main reason is that to actually want to stand for election you have to be borderline insane and over-the-edge nasty. It's no coincidence that nearly all politicians are a singularly unattractive mix of ego, self-belief, power-hunger and a desire to compensate for the fact that they look like a toad by making other people's lives miserable. What other kind of person would choose to validate their existence by having a ballot cast on it?

The foul compulsions of professional politicians were well understood in ancient Athens. There, most elections were decided by sortition. Jobs were attributed by lot – with pebbles pulled out of special randomising machines ensuring that they really did have a government of the people, for the people and by the people, and that those sick enough to actually want to rule never dominated politics. Almost as soon as the system was put in place the Athenians began to develop the most advanced society the world had ever seen – and went on to invent central heating, maps and hula hoops. Achievements that our own corrupt parliamentary democracy can only look on in wonder.

85

Bathe in the Ganges

Those of a spiritual persuasion may have religious reasons for immersing themselves in India's biggest open sewer, but otherwise the waters of the Hindi holy river are to be avoided at all costs. The 1,557-mile-long stretch of disease-ridden water plays host to the combined pollution of several of the world's biggest and dirtiest cities, endless chemical waste and thousands of human and animal corpses. There's a small chance that it might absolve your sins. It's almost guaranteed to make you shit until you bleed.

USELESS TRIVIA

▸ The main source of the Ganges is an ice cave under the Gangotri glacier high in the Himalayas. It's currently under threat from global warming and – with cruel irony – from the thousands of religious pilgrims who visit to worship the site every year since they deforest the surroundings for fuel (destroying the subsoil streams that feed the glacier) and then help melt the surface of the glacier with their thousands of cooking fires.

86

Go Grape Picking

....

The idea that it might be fun to go picking grapes and perhaps spend more long hours crushing them with your bare feet is one of the great PR coups of modern times. There's evidence of real genius in the fact that wine growers have convinced so many gullible tourists and guidebook writers that this work is somehow romantic, when really it's little better than playing at slaves: hot, back-breaking and ultimately degrading.

87

Play Golf

....

Golf, as Mark Twain pointed out, is a good walk spoiled, but perhaps, strictly speaking, this is one four-letter word that shouldn't appear in this book. After all, if you play golf on a regular basis, the chances are that you're already dead from the head down. How empty must your days be if you choose to fill them chasing a tiny white sphere around in tastelessly landscaped circles? How bored of life are you that rather than living it you'd prefer to put on a lemon-yellow polyester jumper, clashing trousers and waste your hours hunting for a ball? Especially since, as soon as you find this ball, you are compelled to whack it away again.* It makes as much sense as returning to your own vomit.

USELESS TRIVIA

▸ The first recorded mention of golf comes from a Scottish statute enacted 1457 in order to announce that the game had been banned. It seems it had been annoying people even back then.

---

* *The idiocy of this pursuit was neatly summed up by comedian George Carlin, who commented: 'You hit a ball with a stick, then try and find it. Once you do, you hit it again?!?! You're lucky you found it! Go home!!'*

88

Celebrate Summer Solstice
at Stonehenge

....

The ancient stones huddled together on windswept Salisbury Plain present a perplexing mystery. Hundreds of theories have been put forward for their existence.

Were they, as Edgar Barclay suggested in his 1906 treatise *The Ruined Temple Stonehenge,* a kind of Roman 'youth opportunities scheme' set up to bring together the fractious British tribes in the same way as the Olympics doesn't today?

Does the July 1953 discovery of a carved dagger on one of the stones prove that the architect and builder of the great monument was a roving Mycenean prince?

Do the stones signify, as archaeologist Aubrey Burl offered in 1997, a bit of Breton grandstanding; a monument erected by chieftains from northern France to show their dominance over the land and people of southern England?

Were the stones magically moved there by Merlin? Or did the wizard (*pace* Geoffrey of Monmouth, no less) have people bring them over from Killarus in Ireland on specially designed Bronze Age trucks? Did Queen Boudicca have them set up as her monument? Were they an ancient clock for sages from the lost civilisation of Atlantis? Did aliens put them there for their own inscrutable purpose?

The only thing that is certain is that we know chuff all about the circle's origins and purpose. Oh yes, and that it was erected a good millennium before the first Druids arrived in the UK. Which means that the guys with beards who currently frequent the stones at solstice time have no more clue about the right ceremonies to perform there than you or I. They might chat a lot of impressive-sounding guff about 'oak kings' being overcome by 'holly kings', give themselves mystical names and wave around big swords, but really they might as well be making it up as they go along.

No number of goaty men in rainbow jumpers and women dressed like Stevie Nicks, clattering on bongos, juggling and dribbling on about 'mystical links with our spiritual ancestry' can conceal the fact that the whole annual pilgrimage is a nonsensical charade and ought to be avoided as such.

USELESS TRIVIA

▸ The latest archaeological evidence from Stonehenge suggests that ancient people were never there in the summer. This theory is based on analysis of large numbers of pigs' teeth around the site. Most of the teeth belonged to pigs more than six months but less than one year old. Since domestic pigs in the Neolithic period were born in the spring and farrowed once a year, the findings suggest that our ancestors probably took part in a winter solstice ceremony, and that, as Professor Mike Parker Pearson of Sheffield University, who led the project, said: 'We have no evidence that anyone was in the landscape in summer.'

Take that, hippies!

89

Eat Fugu

....

In Western Japan, fugu is known as fuku and given half a chance it will – but not in a good way. Just one of these ugly spiked blowfish contains enough poison to kill 30 people. They're loaded up with tetrodotoxin, a venom that shuts down electrical signalling in nerves and is 1,200 times more deadly than cyanide. Symptoms include numbness of the lips, tongue and fingers; dizziness; slurred speech; a detached sensation of floating; headache; nausea; stomach cramps and pain; muscle weakness; difficulty walking; uncontrollable shitting… All followed by death within a few hours, generally from asphyxiation. An especially nasty twist is that while the poison paralyses most of the body, it doesn't affect the brain, meaning that the victims remain fully conscious throughout their ordeal, aware of every second of pain and the pressing imminence of their death. There is no known antidote.

Fear junkies might find some appeal to this fishy business in that it all sounds damn terrifying – and quite exciting in a dumb playing-Russian-roulette-with-your-dinner kind of way. The reality of eating fugu is far more prosaic, however.

In the countries where it is available, there are scrupulous regulations about the removal of the poison and strict licensing laws which dictate that those who serve the fish have to go through at least three years of training and regularly pass exams, thus making fugu perfectly safe for consumption and enabling tons of the stuff to be gobbled every year. So much, in fact, that stocks of the fish have been severely depleted.

So, yes, it's true that if sliced incorrectly the fish is poisonous and potentially fatal – but nearly all reported deaths are caused by amateur illegal chefs. More normal punters like you and I, who don't have a ready supply of the stuff, have to go to licensed restaurants. There we would have to part with hundreds of pounds for the privilege of eating a meal that is no more interesting than a cheese sandwich – and considerably less tasty. Optimistic foodies may talk of the dish's subtle and elegant flavours, but what that actually means is that the fish is essentially bland and almost flavourless. Reliable critics have described it as being a bit like eating wet, chewy supermarket chicken. But more than fifty times more expensive.

90

Understand the Sound of One Hand Clapping

....

'What is the sound of the single hand?' asked the Zen Master Hakuin in the eighteenth century, and so was born one of the most famous Zen Buddhist koans of all time. 'When two hands are clapped there's a sharp sound,' the old monk observed. 'But when you raise just one,' he wisely pointed out, 'there is neither sound nor smell.' He then wanted to know if that 'is high heaven?'

By thinking over such complex matters, we are told, the Zen student's mind becomes equal to that of an enlightened being. To help them on their way, Zen teachers sometimes ask their students to listen to just one hand when they clap. Or to concentrate on the time when the hands are apart, just before they join. Or to just hold one hand out. What is the sound then, they ask? Concentrate on that! Unlearn hearing nothing!

There is an alternative to these ramblings, however. As Bart Simpson once pointed out, a true understanding of the sound of one hand clapping is easily obtainable: just slap your fingers down against your palm.

► Koans are stories, riddles, questions or statements that usually contain elements beyond rational understanding and are used within the Zen Buddhist tradition to set students along the path to enlightenment and by Westerners who mistake talking bollocks for mystical wisdom.

► Below are a few famous centuries-old koans and some random nonsense invented in no more than two minutes, while also monitoring confusing cricket scores on the internet. Can you tell which are real and which are not? Think on, grasshopper!

A student asked Master Yun-Men: 'Not even a thought has arisen; is there still a sin or not?' Master Yun-Men replied, 'Mount Sumeru!'

A monk said to Tetsugen, his master: 'Can you show me the way to enlightenment?' Tetsugen beat him with his stick and said: 'Cherry blossom'.

A monk asked Dongshan Shouchu: 'What is Buddha?' Dongshan said: 'Three pounds of flax'.

Before embarking on a long journey, a pupil asked his master Katsuhito what he should take with him to help him know the Buddha as he travelled. Katsuhito said nothing.

A young monk asked Zhaozhou: 'What is the meaning of the ancestral teacher's coming from the west?' Zhaozhou replied: 'The cypress tree in front of the hall.'

Gudo and his pupil were dining on Miso soup. When the bowls were filled the pupil asked: 'Master, how will I know I understand Zen?' Gudo emptied the bowl over his head and said: 'This is the knowledge that you seek'.*

---

* *They alternate – the first is true, second false, third true, etc.*

91

Procreate

. . . .

By the time you finish reading this sentence, another seven people will have been born. By the time you've got to the end of this one (especially if I stretch things a bit here) the total will now have reached 21. Freakily, people are being born faster than I can even write these words and you can read them. Go for a cup of tea midway through reading this entry and enough babies to fill an Olympic swimming pool will have been dragged kicking and screaming into the world.

To put that information another way: 237,000 people are born every 24 hours while only 140,000 die.

Scary isn't it?

But not half so scary as looking at the implications of that birth rate spread over the centuries: in 1750, there were 791 million people. In 1800: 978 million. 1850: 1 billion. 1950: 2.5 billion. 2000: 6 billion.

At the time of writing there are 6.6 billion people in the world. We're scheduled to hit 7 billion by 2012. By 2050, there will be 9 billion.

That's 9 billion mouths and anuses. 9 billion tubes on legs

spouting crap at both ends and chewing up more and more of the earth's precious resources. Do you really want to add to this vast and worthless collection of bad haircuts? This all-consuming, all-destroying swarm of useless knowledge, self-regarding angst and greenhouse gas emissions?

Do you really want to bring your child into all that mess? Worse still, do you want your child to interact with it, have sex with it and produce yet more useless yakking mouths and poo-ing bottoms? If you really think your genes are special, cryogenically freezing them is a far better way of preserving them than getting them all mixed up in that lot. Plus that way you won't have to worry about changing nappies, teenage tantrums and paying to send the ungrateful sods through university.

92

Join the 16-Mile High Club in a MiG-25

. . . .

Marketed to the kind of businessmen who like to think they're boundary-pushing and barrier-breaking, a flight to the edge of the earth's atmosphere in a MiG-25 has the cachet of its immense expense, pointless danger and that roaring phallic symbol provided by jet engines thrusting for the stratosphere.

Admittedly, there's a certain amount of bravery in travelling to Russia and going up in a battered old Soviet-era jet. But if you're after that dropping-out-of the-sky kind of thrill, it's cheaper and easier just to fly Aeroflot.

There's also a certain novelty in feeling the effect of G-forces on your face. But that's nothing that can't be achieved with far more dramatic results by holding a leaf blower up to your head and flicking the power to maximum.*

And the edgy business types won't really get to feel like an astronaut as the brochures suggest. Astronauts are scien-

---

* *Try it sometime. The results are really quite unusual.*

tific pioneers pushing the boundaries of knowledge whereas those businessmen are parasite capitalists, piggybacking on the poverty of Russian airmen and burning through their ill-gotten gains in high-octane jet fuel at a rate of 10,000 gallons an hour.

'Flight suit! Oxygen mask! Helmet!' gush the macho promoters of this obscene brand of pointless there-and-straight-back-again travel, promising that you will: Travel faster than thunder! See the curve of the earth! And that: the only things higher than you will be the cosmonauts on the International Space Station and Pete Doherty's fleas!

But no amount of overcompensatory braggadocio about adventure makes up for the tiny cockpits that edge-pushing thrill seekers are actually lumbered with, as they sit cramped up in the nose of the plane while the real pilot occupies another pod ten feet back and does everything he can to forget they're there...

USELESS TRIVIA

▶ This multi-thousand-dollar test of intestinal fortitude burns up more than 5,000 gallons of jet fuel in just over half an hour. If the pilot pushes too far into the upper atmosphere the jet engines will cease to work since the air is too thin for them to push against, and the plane will fall from the air like a brick. Sadly, this rarely happens.

93

Go to the
Glastonbury Festival

Glastonbury is a triumph of paranoia marketing. Every year we're duped into thinking that if we miss these three days of sunshine-soaked rock and roll and love in the mystic Vale of Avalon we'll be missing the biggest cultural event in the galaxy. If you believe the hype, Glastonbury is not only a major confluence of ley lines, it has a magnetic effect upon cool. Everything that is worthwhile, interesting and fashionable will be taking place inside the giant anti-Scouser security fences in this blessed slice of Somerset in early summer. Everyone who is not there is, therefore, by definition, almost certainly not hip and definitely missing out.

The irony in all this hubristic overselling is that very little of real interest has ever happened at Glastonbury. A few bands have played. A few people have taken a few too many drugs. It's rained. And rained and rained. The only truly memorable happenings were a dozen or so people suffering from trench foot in 2005 and a pitched battle between security guards and New Age travellers in 1990.

Otherwise, the reality of the festival is huge toilet queues, warm beer in cardboard cups and stoned Trustafarians trying to tell you 'it's not about the music man', which is a damn good job since so much of the line-up is always dedicated to Coldplay-style mortgage rock and sub-Rolf Harris novelty acts.

The 100,000-plus punters in attendance on the site represent a city the size of Sunderland and, just as in Sunderland, everyone's intent on getting as drunk as they can in order to obliterate the horror of their surroundings. But even Sunderland has the advantage over Glasonbury. At least in the post-industrially blighted northern town the inebriated have homes to go back to and sleep it off in. In Glastonbury there are only cold, generally flooded tents and accompanying hordes of bedless mashed-up vagrants who spend their time making your life as miserable as possible, keeping you awake all night slamming toilet doors, screaming obscenities about the continuing awful weather and busking tuneless Babyshambles songs around a fire they've built from plastic bottles and wrecked clothes.

A night of misery that has an unusually high probability of being capped off when your own tent is washed away in a stream of muddy piss and a drunk student falls on your head.

There is at least a small chance that you will have one moment of near happiness the following morning when the sun briefly comes out, while you're sitting near the ludicrous fake stone circle and the cloacal mud on your clothes finally begins to dry. At which point, seeing you smile, a grizzly, old hippy in a filthy, half-cocked jester's hat will lean over and tell you that it's not as good as it used to be since they put the fence up, it's all gone too commercial and his ticket money would have been better spent travelling somewhere sunny. As he rounds off the conversation by chundering up a hot, wet stew of bean burger, cider and magic mushrooms onto your lap, you will be alarmed to note that you actually agree with what this ruined, tripping fool has told you. And that you still face another 48 hours before you can hope to go to a clean toilet.

94

Hold a House Party

....

Although everyone feels compelled to do it, tidying your home in preparation for a house party is as pointless as buying new trousers before having your legs amputated. Why show pride in your surroundings when you've invited people round to smash them up?

Generally, house parties are to your stuff what cholera is to stomachs – a raging, shitty torrent of disaster. You'll get red wine on the carpet. Your plant pots will be used as ashtrays. Your glasses will be smashed. Your toilets will be soiled. Your records will be scratched (and laughed at). Your valuables will be variously stolen, broken and used as surfaces from which to take badly cut drugs. Ugly people will have sex in your bed. Your speakers will blow, your neighbours will complain, the police will beat people up as they leave. Your hangover the following morning will not be helped by the knowledge that someone has done a poo in your cupboard.

Alternatively, if none of that happens and your property is saved, you still lose. Your party has clearly been rubbish and you will suffer social death.

▸ MySpace, Facebook and other social networking sites have opened up a whole new realm of horrors for those who have been persuaded to provide house parties. The phenomenon first hit the headlines in the UK when Rachael Bell went into hiding having advertised a 'trash the average family-sized house all-night party' on her MySpace page and more than 200 turned up and proceeded to wreck Rachael's mother's clothes, urinate on beds and carpets, spray graffiti on the walls and vomit just about everywhere.

Then, in February 2008, a 15-year-old girl's innocent sleepover in Worthing turned into a similarly unfortunate drug-fuelled orgy when more than 100 people led by a group calling itself 'The Facebook Republican Army' turned up, drenched the carpet in beer, had sex on the washing machine and fed drugs to the dog. Less than a month later, 17-year-old Sarah Ruscoe made the papers when a whopping 2,000 people turned up at a party at her parents' house in Devon. Pictures were ripped off walls, windows and mirrors were smashed and chandeliers and doors were damaged. Repairs at the Grade II listed building were expected to cost more than £2,000. Revellers were eventually cleared away from the house by police using dogs, and her older brother Stephen had to leave the premises in an air-ambulance.

The exception that proves the rule about the modern nightmare of house parties is Australian 16-year-old Corey Delane, who shot to fame after 500 people turned up at his parents home and did £10,000 worth of damage, but he still declared it 'the best party ever' and went on to start a lucrative career as an events organiser. His popularity was not universal, however, as was proved when a website featuring a game centred around the premise of 'slapping Corey down the street' received more than a million hits in a month.

95

Re-watch Your Favourite Childhood TV Programmes

. . . .

The many people who attempt to clog up so many of your precious moments on earth by recounting their memories of the TV programmes they used to love back when they were tiny are blights. No matter that they were unable to even feed themselves when they first watched those multicoloured delights, or that their critical faculties were no more developed than the average dog or *Daily Mail* journalist. They just *have* to tell you all about Jamie and his magic torch and how they innocently missed its innuendo first time around, before they go on to repeat untrue urban legends about Roger the cabin boy, Dylan the druggy rabbit and Zippy and Bungle's home habits.

These crimes have now been compounded by the release of so many children's series on DVD and by the legions of self-help writers who inform us it will be 'soul-nurturing' to watch them. But the humiliating truth is that what's really wanted from watching those programmes is one's childhood back again. Innocence; no worries more pressing than when you're next going to have a poo; someone appearing every so often with a plate of biscuits and a nice refreshing glass of Ribena. But, as Thomas Wolfe warned, you can never go home again. If you return to those old programmes your memories will be forever tarnished. You'll see the strings, the cracks, the flimsy backdrops, and you'll all too clearly understand the logical impossibility of the moon being made from a button or of Paul Daniels being entertaining, with or without an alien magician called Wizbit.

The only way to truly get back the happy artlessness of childhood is to go senile. But then you'll be too busy watching *Countdown* to worry about infantile nostalgia.

96

Busk in Prague

··

If you have to busk, Prague is sold to us as the ultimate place
to do it. Never mind that that's a recommendation almost on
a par with Chernobyl being the ultimate place to contract
leukaemia, or Iraq being the ultimate place to get your legs
and arms blown off, the merits of Prague for such an activity
are highly dubious anyway.

Perhaps some of this confusion is owed to the ancient city's
position as the capital of Bohemia; a fact that has seemingly
entranced a generation of people that call themselves travellers instead of tourists into Prague, and made its ancient
streets busier than the LA freeway. These roll-up-smoking,
beret-wearing, absinthe-quaffing hipsters have inevitably
destroyed the authenticity they crave, turning the city into a
turreted version of Blackpool instead of an edgy retreat from
capitalism. This craven desire for easy money is best exempli-
fied by the throngs of buskers who compete for ears and space
on the Charles Bridge with refrigerator-magnet stalls and
sketch artists. Do not become a guidebook cliché and aural
irritant by joining them. Most of all do not sing *that* perennial

busker-favourite song by The Verve. If you really were a 'Lucky Man', you wouldn't be sitting on the hard ground singing for coins, would you?

USELESS TRIVIA

▸ So great is the plague of buskers in the centre of Prague that authorities have made it illegal to start caterwauling there without a licence.

97

Go Shopping in Milan

....

Milan used to be the spiritual home of Italian fascism. Now it's where many of the world's leading fashion houses are based and have their flagship stores. The major difference between now and the 1920s being that Mussolini and his mob of peacock-feather wearing gangsters generally sported more subtle outfits.

Filling up your wardrobe in Milan is especially foolish because nothing ages less gracefully than fashion. Today's slick strides are tomorrow's loon pants. That trendy hat will date you as surely as a flat cap does your grandfather. Now you think you are the smartest person on the block; when your children see your picture in 20 years' time they'll have the same reaction we have to Noddy Holder and his tartan-flared friends in Slade. Following fashion is as foolish as following that burning line of powder leading to a box of TNT in Bugs Bunny cartoons – and just as likely to explode in your face. Only with less amusing results for yourself. Milan, as the cutting edge of haute couture, is the stabbingly silly apex of this absurdity.

Don't buy into the much-put-about idea that you might be able to find a brand to reflect your personal values, either. Unless, that is, your values include taking people for suckers, the exploitation of sweatshop labour and gold-plating handbag straps. Otherwise donning haute couture just makes you appear a gullible fool.

98

Join a
Re-enactment Society

....

The issue with re-enactment societies isn't that you will look
and feel stupid and have to interact with fields and fields
full of geeks (even though you will), it's that they don't use
bullets. If those aiming to recreate 'authentic' battles used real
loaded guns, the world would not just be relieved of a few
idiots. A useful corrective would also be applied to those who
think that going into battle is all about putting on a silly hat
and shouting 'charge'. Because war without weapons is like
shaving without razors. That's to say, it's not war at all and
useless to indulge in.

When those who have had to fight in wars relive their
memories, they don't chunter on about uniforms, haircuts
and appropriate camouflage as per the re-enacters. They tell
of watching their friends die, of dreadful wounds, of trauma,
of rage, of horror...

Battles are not fun days out to be enjoyed with picnics.
Reliving them for entertainment and without weapons is
as perverse as dressing up to enact medical operations

(performed with rubber scalpels) or re-treading famous funerals (without a body or burial). Especially since if you really want to experience the fun and excitement of real war, a far simpler and faster way to do it is available: shoot your own face off.

99

Pimp Your Ride

....

'Pimping your ride' is street slang for adding chrome wheels, flashing lights and obscenely loud stereo speakers to your automobile, so that people you pass on the street know you're a knobhead without having to go to the trouble of talking to you.

100

Stroll Down Las Ramblas in Barcelona

....

Rambla means riverbed in Arabic, but years ago the old river from which this famous street took its name was drained off. It has now been replaced by a sewer. This long pedestrianised zone is touted everywhere as the place to visit in Barcelona and the resultant overcrowding is just one of the reasons it's so unpleasant to walk along. Others include: the swarms of pickpockets who prey on this seething mass of punters; the braying, puking, stag-party scrums; the prostitutes who drift around them like the proverbial flies around shit; the hen-party gaggles, cackling, wearing balloons shaped (hilariously!) like penises, swigging sangria from boot-shaped glasses; the street cafés selling this sangria at €8 a glass; the deathly boring living statue street-theatre; the mime artists who swear at you loudly in five different languages if you refuse to give them any money for troubling you with their cretinous clown routines; the artists doing portraits that look nothing like their subjects; the fact that the pictures look nothing like their subjects comes as a blessed relief; the not-so-hot breakdancers; the heat; the hopeless crippled beggars that no one will help; the helpless caged animals, crying, whining, twittering in fear; the Americans asking the way to the Gaudí museum; the mystery of why so many stalls are selling Mexican hats; the dangers of walking there after dark; the equal dangers of walking there in daylight; the growing realisation that you can't avoid being caught up in this torrent of shit because of its central location and that your holiday in Barcelona is therefore going to be ruined.

Inexplicably, the otherwise sound poet Federico García Lorca declared Las Ramblas 'the only street in the world which I wish would never end.' But of course, end it does, fittingly enough punctuated by a gaudy and tasteless statue of infamous mass murderer Christopher Columbus.

101

Dance Until Dawn

....

When aliens finally visit this planet and start to probe, enslave and rule over us, there is one human custom that will confuse them even more than fox-hunting, cricket and the popularity of gobby Radio 1 DJ Chris Moyles combined: dancing. Why, they will wonder, are all these people running on the spot and flailing their arms about so strangely? Why do repeated thudding and whistling sounds make them do it all the more enthusiastically? Why such intense flashing lights? Wherefore The Village People?

Most other exercise – although undignified and generally to be avoided – can be rationalised to the extent that it gets you somewhere and/or trains up reflexes. Dancing, in contrast, is good only for cutting peculiar shapes in the sky with your hands and making you sweat all over your best pulling clothes. Our new galactic overlords will therefore probably conclude – much as most human anthropologists have – that dancing is actually a primitive, and unusually ineffective, mating-ritual. And if that is the case, dancing until dawn defeats the object entirely. Contrary to the urgings of the To-Do lists, expending all that energy and losing all that dignity for an entire night without enticing a sex partner is a failure, not something to aim for. The best case scenario for dancing is doing it for less than five minutes, pulling, and then leaving all that noise and commotion behind for a night of genuine passion. If you're still on the dance-floor when the sun comes up you might as well never have bothered.

Some enthusiasts might try to argue that dancing isn't simply about sex. They will claim to take genuine delight in jumping up and down on the same square foot of ground for the entire night and if you ask them why, they will happily gurn that 'It's all about the music, man.' These people are on drugs and their opinions should be measured accordingly. They would probably enjoy bopping along to the percussive beats of nuclear bombs dropping around them at the beginning of End Times. What's more, while the dance fiends' narcotic intake is entirely their business, the fact that they need to take so many illegal substances in order to keep on keeping on until the sun comes up surely proves the point. It isn't something anyone in their right mind would do.

102

Oktoberfest

....

Oktoberfest, the gigantic beer-drinking binge in the Bavarian city of Munich (which, confusingly, begins in mid-September), claims to be the largest fair in the world. Certainly it generates some mind-boggling and belly-popping statistics. The event attracts more than 5 million visitors, employs 12,000 people (1,600 of whom are the always popular barmaids) and produces 1,000 tons of refuse. During the three weeks 400,000 sausages, 600,000 chickens and 6.1 million litres of beer are consumed. And it's this latter figure that accounts for the curious local phenomenon of *bierleichen* ('beer corpses'): the thousands of catatonically sozzled punters who have to be cleared from the tents every day to receive medical attention.

Offensive as all that drinking and gluttony might be to those of a temperate disposition, most of it can be described as reasonably harmless and the event always remains remarkably peaceful – if puke-drenched. The real objection and the true evil of the event is far more disturbing. The great crime of Oktoberfest is that it encourages, and actively promotes, Oom-pah music.

Those unfamiliar with the horrors of Oom-pah music should think of 'The Birdie Song' played by drunken men wearing lederhosen, and they will begin to scratch the surface of this deeply disfiguring wound on the face of European culture. Those who have had the displeasure of hearing an Oom-pah band in full spate, meanwhile, will understand why Germans genuinely and unironically enjoy the music of David Hasselhoff. Compared to the average contemporary Oom-pah band, even the Hoff is a musical genius. A fact that not even five litres of high-quality Bavarian beer can conceal.

USELESS TRIVIA

▸ During the 2004 Oktoberfest, the queues for the toilets grew so long that the police had to be brought in to regulate the motions of the agonised beer-laden punters.

103

Read Another Book of Lists…

....

Aren't you just sick to the back teeth of people telling you what to do? Of grinding sarcasm and haughty superiority? In what way does knowing you've taken any advice from these self-appointed arbiters validate your life? Not at all, I'd say. In fact, I'd advise you to stop reading this book right away. There's really nothing more that its author can tell you…

Thanks

....

For stories, inspiration, inspiring commissions and invaluable advice:

Eloise Millar, Susan Smith, Ian Marshall and Anna Valentine, David Riding, Becky Hatch, Tim Harcourt, Sarah Crown, Robin Deitch, Alex Needham and the person (who shall remain nameless) who first got my blood boiling by telling me I hadn't lived until I'd read all of *Ulysses*...

APPENDIX 1

A note on selection criteria

....

All entries concern suggestions that have been selected from bona fide lists and self-help books.

There's only very dubious value in naming and shaming each of the authors individually in relation to each entry, not least because so many of these entries are cited as great things to do by multiple sources. I'm also worried that if I did cite individuals, the bastards might sue me.

It is worth including a list of *Sod That*'s main inspirations, however. Primarily to prove that I'm not making this shit up. I really did spend months reading self-help books* and someone, somewhere, really does think that you should eat rotting shark and throw yourself out of a plane. There's also the possibility that plenty of readers will disagree with the conclusions drawn in this book. In which case you might actually find plenty of ideas in these books appealing:

---

* *This means that I've spent an awful lot of the time reading the type of books that tell you that you need to 'begin acting as if you trusted', 'kindness is a powerful medicine' and that polluting the planet by flying to the edge of space is not half so dangerous as it is 'kewl'. So if the tone ever sounds sneering, it's only because of extreme provocation.*

Make the Most Of Your Time On Earth, 1000 Ultimate Travel Experiences, A Rough Guide To The World – Rough Guides

101 Things to Do Before You Die – Richard Horne

101 Things to Buy Before You Die – Charlotte Williamson and Maggie Davis

The Guardian Guide to Adventure – the *Guardian*

Unforgettable Things to Do Before You Die – Steve Watkins and Clare Jones

2,001 Things to Do Before You Die – Dane Sherwood

100 Things to Do Before You Die (Plus a Few to Do Afterwards) – New Scientist

This Diary Will Change Your Life 2008 – Benrik Ltd

1,000 Places to See Before You Die – Patricia Schultz

The Secrets of Happiness, 100 Ways To True Fulfilment – Ben Renshaw

The Goddess Guide – Gisele Scanlon

Ultimate Gift Experiences – Steve Shipside

Goddess, Be the Woman You Want to Be – Elizabeth Wilson

The Manly Man Manual, 100 Brilliant Ideas for Being a Top Bloke – Steve Shipside

2DO Before I Die, The Do-It-Yourself Guide to the Rest of Your Life – Michael Ogden and Chris Day

Forbes to the Limits, Pushing Yourself to the Edge in Adventure and in Business – James M Clash

Websites

www.seebeforeyoudie.net
www.superviva.net
www.2dobeforeidie.com
www.your100things.com
www.wanderlist.com/beforedeath
www.my50.com
http://travel.agoda.com/
http://www.grantthorpe.com/100-things-to-do.htm
http://202things.blogspot.com/
http://kitchen-parade-veggieventure.blogspot.com/

In the end I elected not to borrow any entries from the most out-there lists. I'm sure you don't need to be warned about going down the water slide in Keighley for instance, since chances are that you would rather die than go there anyway. Certainly that's true if you're anything like Martin Newell*, who probably provided the poor, old, rundown town's biggest bid for immortality when he wrote: 'I'll tell you once and I'll tell you briefly, I don't want to go to Keighley.' Besides, it seems unfair to further pick on a place that is so oft-maligned – and any other similarly already recognised crap towns.** Equally importantly, it struck me that far more worthy targets were lists that some of us could potentially take seriously. Lists that are supposed to appeal to all of us and goad us into actions we otherwise (quite rightly!) wouldn't bother taking. Those arbitrary life targets that there's actually no real need to aim for...

---

* A legendary English renaissance man, aka 'The Wild Man of Wivenhoe', the lead singer of bands like Plod, The Brotherhood Of Lizards and The Stray Trolleys, poet, respected author and columnist for the East Anglian Daily Times.

** Fictional places were also off-limits for obvious reasons. This meant, sadly, that a fantastic list of 'Things to Do in Hooterville Before You Die' was also ignored.

Finally, a small admission. The instruction to 'panic' (entry 71) doesn't directly appear in any list I've found. However, the implication that we should is all around the entire time. Especially if you've had the misfortune to watch Fox news or listen to announcements by that sinister organisation that spends more time and effort than any other trying to goad us, the people, into doing things we really don't want to do: the government. There's also a brilliantly entertaining sub-genre of lists advising on things you really should pack before Armageddon, nuclear holocaust and the inevitable and you-better-believe-it's-imminent bio-terrorism attack that will shortly destroy your small town in the middle of an isolated part of America... Which seemed like qualification enough to include things under the 'panic' umbrella. Not least because the author was keen to nudge those with *Dad's Army* TV nostalgia to start shouting 'Don't Panic' inside their heads. Anyway...

A Note on Statistics

The platitudes about fun and worry in entry 71 are half-remembered and almost certainly misquoted. I can't substantiate those claims about cancer and heart attacks either. I read them somewhere, I think, but have to admit that there's a small chance I made them up; as do most other journalists and wannabe writers, especially when it comes to giving you medical facts and telling you what to do with your body. Never believe them unless they present you with real evidence. Authors and newspapermen might be fantastic in bed because of the effects of sitting at a desk all day on their sexual middle regions; they might also be undoubtedly the coolest people you will ever meet and they might also be a wonderfully fantastic laugh in the pub due to the increased knowledge of everything that their profession brings them and the medical effects of news facts on the lymphatic wit glands, but really, they're deceptive scum.

That said, there is some fun to be had with numbers. And I can* at least back up all other statistical assertions made in the book. I'd forgive you for not believing me now, so will note a few of the more interesting sources below. Chasing these up will also provide you with yet more evidence as to why it might not be a good idea to go and do these things. If you follow up the 'Take a Shower in a Waterfall' (entry 68) figures and buy *Death in Yosemite* meanwhile, you might never go to a US national park again. Which would be a shame because they are quite pretty. Even if the food tends to be awful.

ROLLERCOASTER DEATHS
From 1987 to mid-2004, 64 amusement-park ride fatalities were documented by the US Consumer Product Safety Commission.

For a terrifying overview of the dangers of funfairs, have a look at **http://www.rideaccidents.com/** and http://saferparks.org/

For more info on British funfair accidents see: **http://news.bbc.co.uk/1/hi/uk/905558.stm**

In the year 2000, there were 14 injuries and three deaths. Ouch.

BIRTH STATISTICS
The figures in entry 91 come from a combined reading of a 2004 UN world population report and the slightly sinister, but endlessly fascinating, CIA World Factbook. At the time of writing, an online version is available here: **https://www.cia.gov/library/publications/the-world-factbook/**

---

* Or, well, I think I can.

NEIGHBOUR STATISTICS

The facts and figures about neighbours from hell are mainly culled from the UK Home Office. More information here: **http://www.homeoffice.gov.uk/about-us/news/asbo-house-powers**.

If you're browsing the web, you might also want to have a look at the website specifically dedicated to 'Neighbours From Hell': **http://www.nfh.org.uk/**. It's enough to make you think that taking up residence on Tuvalu and waiting for it to all to sink might not be such a bad idea after all...

READING STATISTICS

Statistics about bookclubs and *Ulysses* were both culled from the fantastic website of the National Literary Trust: **http://www.literacytrust.org.uk/Database/stats/readingstats.html**.

Interestingly, this site also suggests that in the UK reading is more popular than sex, being noted down as an important activity by 79% of respondents to a survey as opposed to the (highly suspicious) figure of 69% for sex. Also worth noting is the assertion that far more men than women read while on the toilet.

APPENDIX 2

Top Fives

....

For the benefit of those who feel that life is too short even to read this book:

CHAPTER

What Not to Read
The Bible		79
Ulysses		39
Kama Sutra		2
Wordsworth – 'Daffodils'		64
Robert Browning – 'Pheidippides'		40

Sports to Avoid
Marathon running		40
Zorbing		65
Ski-ing		29
Parachuting		4
Dirtboarding		30

Things Not to Eat
Hákarl: rotting shark flesh		14
Fugu: poisonous, but otherwise dull, fish		89
Kopi Luwak: jungle weasel turd coffee		35
Hillsides (see dirtboarding)		30
Someone else's vomit		21

not2dobeforeidie.co.uk

....

Have you regretted running a marathon? Have you been persuaded to read a terrible book? Have you realised that dolphins may not appreciate you swimming with them? Have you eaten something you shouldn't have on someone else's bad advice? Did you have an awful time at Glastonbury? Has your dream holiday turned into a nightmare? Can't be arsed to read *Ulysses* either?

While writing this book, it occurred to me that it might be fun to share a few suggestions for things not to bother doing, stories about things you might have been persuaded to do that ended up being rubbish and general gripes about the selfishness of self-help culture.

So! I'd be delighted if you were to visit not2dobeforeidie.co.uk and tell me your stories. And even if you don't have anything to share yourself, feel free drop in to laugh along with – or indeed at – everyone else.

I'll also be building up a comprehensive list of all the stuff none of us want to do half as much as self-help writers might think... All ideas gratefully received at: **http://www.not2do beforeidie.co.uk**

Okay, advert over.

Blank Pages

....

Please feel free to fill in your own things that you can't be bothered to do. Or don't, as the fancy takes you. You can also use these pages to collect your memories of things you've been told to do in the past and really haven't enjoyed, to look back on next time you feel pressurised into embarking on a 'fun' run in a chicken suit, throwing yourself out of a plane or similar.

Alternatively, use these pages to create your own To-Do list ghetto. Simply cut out all the 'Top 50 before you die' lists that assault you from newspapers, magazines and books and glue them into these pages where they will be neutralised and trouble you no more.

Index

....